Mists of *Mackinac*

FORGOTTEN FOLKLORE, FANTASY, AND PHENOMENA

JOAN ST. JOHN

WITH ROBB KACZOR

Published by StarQuest International Inc.
First Print Edition: September 2012

ISBN-10: 0-9883359-2-1
ISBN-13: 978-0-9883359-2-9

Cover and Formatting by Streetlight Graphics

For information contact:
StarQuest International Inc.
PO Box 1745, Ann Arbor, MI 48103
Tel: 1-800-275-5626
E-mail: info@starquestinternationalinc.com

All photos taken by the authors except where credited otherwise.

I dedicate this book to my husband, who continues to profess his confidence in my abilities, cheering me onward, fueled by his ardent desire to be the trailing spouse.

Also to my children, their loving hearts, devotion, beautiful smiles and need for daily feeding and care have kept me grounded in my human reality as I fly in and out of body to do my work.

Table of Contents

Mackinac
Island

British Landing Rd

State Rd

Airport

StoneCliff Rd

Fort Holmes

Great
Turtle
Park

West Bluff Rd

Spring St

Fort
Mackinac

Huron Rd

Cadotte Ave

Market St

Boat Docks

Main St

① PINE COTTAGE
② THE CHATEAU LORRAINE
③ SMALL POINTS COTTAGE
④ STONECLIFF ESTATES
⑤ THE GRAND HOTEL
⑥ THE ISLAND HOUSE
⑦ ARCH ROCK
⑧ SKULL CAVE
⑨ ST. ANNE'S CEMETERY
⑩ POST CEMETERY
⑪ MACKINAC ISLAND CEMETERY

Foreword

THE QUESTION I AM OFTEN asked is why did I decide to become a professional psychic.

After all, it is not exactly a main stream profession. For most, it conjures up the image of a gypsy caravan, or a neon sign blaring in a store front window on the boardwalk, where sitting in a dimly lit room, tarot cards spread, a reader speaks in a language of mystical words and offers strange predictions.

My life started out as with most people, a college degree, marriage, children, PTA meetings, a typical mini-van driving soccer mom. No signs of anything out of the ordinary, nothing on the outside, at least. But dig a little deeper and you will find small occurrences popping in and out of my life since childhood. Certain people entered who left a bit of magic, a shining light in the darkness that I followed without even realizing it.

My first recollection was Rosie. With a cackle of a laugh and a twinkle in her eye, she appeared crone like back when I was a child. A deck of playing cards was magic in her hands! She would turn over a simple card and tell my future. At twelve I was transfixed. Her predictions had an air of mystery, but somehow they always seemed to come true. I kept in touch with Rosie long after I was grown, until my letters to her were returned with the word "deceased"

1

scrawled across the envelope. She was my first example of what was possible, and I speak with her still.

I remember my encounter with the book "The Search for Bridey Murphy", by Morey Bernstein. It was being used as a wedge under a bookcase to keep it level. I rescued it and proceeded to devour it for two days nonstop during my 13th year. To this day it maintains its prominence on my bookshelf. It was my first encounter with the concept of reincarnation. A voice within me seemed to yell out gleefully, "the nuns are wrong!" ...a sacrilegious thought, but the concept resonated with me. I didn't believe in hell anyway.

Two events years later prompted me further. The spirit possession of my brother, and my surprising ability to communicate with the spirit and release my brother from its grip, and the death of a very dear friend, who made his spiritual presence known to me, after he died, just as he said he would, led me into the world of psychic mediumship.

Venturing into predictive readings just seemed to happen. Not so much as sensing what would occur, but knowing with certainty, and having the confidence to say so, out loud. It did not seem strange to look at someone and know things about their past, present and future. Sometimes a movie played in my head, staring a person and showing me occurrences in their life, other times I would hear a voice telling me what they were going to do, and other times without any logical reason, I would just know.

There has always been much controversy regarding prognosticative readings. It brings out both fear and curiosity. There are some whos' religious beliefs shy away from those that can see future options, and some even consider it the work of the "devil". Certainly intention plays a large part in future predictions. The good of all, must always be at the forefront of the readers' mind. Predicting the future can be seen as a way to show what options lay ahead. A road map, if you will. Others may see it as viewing ones fate. I believe we always have the free will to make our own choices. I see a predictive reading as a tool to assist in our lives. A reading shows us the options that lay ahead, and it is up to us to decide to go that route or not. I choose to see it as the ability to look ahead in the book of life. By seeing what lays ahead helps us avoid obstacles and provide the ability to make better and more informed choices about our lives. Knowing what the options are offers us the advantage of foresight. And can't we all use a little of that!

Predictive readings unveil the options open to us in various areas of our lives. It is up to you to choose which to manifest in order to achieve the dreams and goals you set for yourself. Life offers a wide array of opportunities, as well as consequences. I can see what is available in the future, but the decision to choose an option that leads to an opportunity, or to avoid a path is up to you. Each path taken is a personal choice based on your wants and needs at the time. The future is not etched in stone. We are endowed with free will and our choices are our own responsibility. Of course there are consequences to every action; predictive readings assist in showing you the choices as well as the consequence of each.

On a spirit level, the options presented to us come with the purpose of accomplishing a soul lesson and satisfies our desire to learn it. Do not judge yourself too harshly by the choices you make. Your spirit knows the reason for each decision, even if your conscious self is not ready to see it.

As a clairvoyant I provide psychic reading that offers the opportunity to see what lies ahead within the options available to you, allowing you to view the pros and cons of your decisions. I teach my clients how to use intuition for their highest good, as I believe everyone has a degree of psychic ability and in many cases abilities can be increased beyond expectations. Whereas not everyone will have the same level of skill, just like not everyone will have the ability to be a concert pianist, but they can learn to plink out a simple tune on the piano. It is a matter of honing the level of ability one has in order to define and refine ourselves. My works spans many areas including, predictive readings, personality profiling, pet readings, Spirit Talk-the ability to speak to the subconscious of a living person, law enforcement, past life readings, psychic home inspections-the ability to psychically inspect a house for home buyers, and communicating with spirit, and offers help to the many seeking answers to the questions that weigh heavy on their hearts.

This life is an extraordinary journey of love and learning, psychic ability is a wonderful layer of cosmic color to add to our vision of ourselves, our world and the afterlife.

Preface

THERE ARE MANY PLACES THAT harbor ghosts. This book is about one such place and the ghosts we have encountered there. Filled with a history of spirit activity and hauntings, stories of lost loves, sad demises, and folklore that go back hundreds of years, Mackinac Island is an exceptional place.

There is an abundance of knowledge available to us from the universe and using the ability to communicate with those on the other side, whether loved ones or higher level souls we can attain this knowledge, gain peace and tranquility, reach our highest potential by garnering information we would not otherwise have access to. Unconditional love is offered as well as help, on our journey through this life.

I communicate with spirits offering a connection with things far greater than our present reality. The messages are through me, not of me. I am simply a vessel for their information. It is through this connection we come to learn and understand what happens after death and the reasons some spirits linger among us.

Several years ago I met Robb Kaczor, a paranormal investigator, offering me the opportunity to experiment with ghost hunting. My ability as a psychic medium, combined with Robb's expertise, and interest in Mackinac

Island history made this book a reality.

The only way to describe Robb besides his ever present curiosity and scrutiny of paranormal events is that he is a powerful looking bear of a man, an Indiana Jones of the ghost hunting world. Robb has been investigating paranormal phenomena worldwide for over ten years, logging a multitude of hours reviewing ghost video and EVP evidence. Soft spoken and extremely knowledgeable, he takes an honest and open view of ghost hunting and unlike many others in the field does not reach for false evidence.

Robb is a professional "debunker" and his expertise is called upon by many paranormal investigation groups throughout the world to review paranormal evidence. He finds just as much enjoyment in finding the reasons for a false haunt as discovering evidence of a legitimate experience, as both are helpful to those seeking to document their evidence.

His interest in the paranormal began with the death of and subsequent spirit communication with his grandfather leading him to spend much of his teenage years in cemeteries, fascinated by the lore and stories the headstones told. He happily labels himself a true taphophile. Taphophiles are those individuals who love visiting cemeteries, often seen taking pictures of gravestones, performing gravestone rubbings, and picking up litter around the grounds, due to a high respect and interest for cemeteries. They can easily be spotted by the large smiles on their faces and looks of glee and wonder, as they come upon an interesting find. They generally have more of a skip in their steps while in a cemetery than any other place, and can easily be distinguished from mourners by their cameras, notebooks and other paraphernalia.

Robb has studied the various carvings and engravings on headstones throughout the world. Specific symbols extol the personal beliefs of the people there. Each gravestone tells a story, and it is different for each culture. For instance a bee in America symbolizes the bounty of Christ, whereas a bee in Japan represents the freedom of the soul.[1] You can tell many things about a person by their headstone, their level of affluence, their belief system, what clubs they belonged to, personal interests and hobbies, as seen on modern day headstones, as well as the migration of various family members as some stones with no death date indicate the individual moved away prior to death.

Family plots allow for the study of genealogy. Headstones are also indicative of societal changes; the early 1900's shows a simplistic style whereas the newer ones show a more personal representation of the individuals' life.

Robb agreed to lend his expertise in the field of paranormal investigations to this book. His information in the Ghost Hunting chapters is a must read for anyone interested in experiencing the thrill of the paranormal on their own. Take his words seriously as the uninitiated can be in for more than they bargained for by entering the spirit realm unprepared.

This book transports you back in time through ancient legends and folklore, and opens the door to explore the many paranormal phenomena on Mackinac Island.

The ghost stories have been told for generations, rather than simply retelling old stories, this book, the first of its kind offers the reader actual channeled communications with the spirits residing at Mackinac Island. Mist of

Mackinac explores the paranormal activity occurring there today and offers the ability to take an accurate guided ghost tour of your own, by providing the correct tools for you to carry out your own ghost hunting adventure!

*"There is a doorway to our psychic awareness.
It offers knowledge from a higher vibration,
along with abilities and pathways never anticipated.*

*My doorway did not open
with tentative trepidation or years of study,
but with a mighty force—a gust of cosmic wind."*

-Joan StJohn-

The Beginning:

THE MYSTERY THAT SHROUDS MACKINAC Island began long ago with folk tales told by those who first settled in this mystical place. There is a beautiful native legend explaining the creation of Mackinac Island considered by the original Native American settlers, The Ojibwa, the first land created on earth.

According to Ojibwa tradition, Mackinac Island is a sacred place populated by the first people and was home to the Great Spirit Gitchi Manitou. Its location in the center of the Great Lakes waterway, made it easily accessible and it became a tribal gathering place. Native Americans traveling the Straits region likened the shape of the island to that of a turtle's back and named it Michilimackinac, Land of the Great Turtle. It is said, once the Europeans came, these early visitors fled the Island to dwell in the Northern Lights.

"In the beginning, the Great Hare called Mich-i-bou, Father of all, sat with all his creatures on the surface of the water. It is said that the wife of Mich-i-bou bore him many children. One day as she was about to deliver his thousandth child, she had a dream that the unborn child demanded a solid place on which to stand. When she told her husband, he was puzzled, but at last he decided to create a place. Diving beneath the water, he brought up a grain of sand from

the bottom. Holding it in his hand, he blew upon it until it became Mackinac Island. He set it afloat and here the first man was born."

The Chippewa tell of fishing in these very waters long ago, before there was such an island. And then, they said, there came a great fog which shrouded the Straits of Mackinac for three suns. When it rose there lay the island with all of its trees and blooming flowers. It was at that time that Git-chi-Man-i-tou came to stay.

For many moons no one dared venture near. But finally they came to timidly offer gifts of wampum and other treasures to do him honor. In return he filled their canoes with fish and their lands with game. It was he who gave their chiefs the gift of speech, the warriors' strong arms, and the arrow makers' skill in working the flint. But one day the white man came. Then seeing the harm wrought upon his people, Git-chi-Man-i-tou fled in anger and sorrow to the frozen north as the caribou had done before him to live forever in the flickering flames of the Northern Lights."

—Lore of the Great Turtle by Dirk Gringhuis[2]

There is a history to everything on this earth; for nothing is without its past. It is through the past that we learn of our ancestors, the origins of our beliefs and where we are likely headed in our future. Mackinac Island is such a place. It provides a rich source of history as well as an extraordinary example of paranormal phenomena, a topic that in recent years has gained in popularity and acceptance. This book offers a look at the past in the form of folklore, legends, ghosts, spirits, apparitions and other supernatural phenomena. Voices of the dead whispering their stories, sharing glimpses of lives long gone, affirming the existence of something more than just our present reality, are plentiful here on Mackinac Island.

Other books have been written about this historic island, but none encompass the folklore, fantasy and supernatural phenomena. Mists of Mackinac uncovers the possibilities of how the past connects with the present on Mackinac Island, and offers the tools to enable you to conduct your own paranormal investigation and discover for yourself the mysteries of this magical place.

It is our pleasure to share with you the opportunity to explore for yourself the Island and all its mysteries, and provide the tools for your own investigative adventures. Read on and enjoy this one of a kind experience. Listen carefully and you too can hear it speak! We look forward to seeing you there!

For those of you interested in investigating any of the spirit activity on Mackinac Island, I have added, with thanks to Robb Kaczor, a ghost hunting guide at the end of this book.

Happy Hunting!

Introduction

AM A PSYCHIC MEDIUM. I can see things before they happen. I can hear and see ghosts and other non-physical beings. At times I allow them to take over my body. My voice and mannerisms then reflect their personality, as their words come out of my mouth. To some of you, this may appear strange or bizarre; to others it holds a fascinating curiosity, for me it was an unexpected event. I remember clearly the thought, resonating loudly as it filled my mind, after my first trance channeling experience, *"It is about time I remembered how to do this."*

Twenty years have passed and I continue to "do this", with extreme accuracy and with the heartfelt desire to bring to others this amazing connection. It offers healing to those seeking the comforting knowledge that their loved ones are at peace and content on the other side. It answers questions that would otherwise go unheard. My ability to hear the voices of victims' and visualize crime scenes brings to law enforcement officials a rare assist in solving crimes, aiding in closure to families devastated by traumatic loss of a loved one. I have experienced many unique and intriguing situations as a professional psychic medium, whether offering closure for loved ones lost, helping with difficult life decisions, paranormal investigations, and hearing the voices of the dead helping to solve their own murders. I enter the lives of people from all walks of life, leaving behind a trail of light, assisting them on their life journey.

I offer no reason why I can communicate with spirits, why it works, or how. I continue to be amazed along with my clients. Some may give long and lengthy explanations, as to why this is at all possible, but I feel none is needed. I believe everyone has some form of psychic ability. There are many stories of average people getting a "feeling" and reacting to it. Such as slamming on the brakes, without knowing why, only to have a deer suddenly run in front of their car. Or refusing to get on an airplane, because of an indescribable "bad feeling", and then discovering the plane had crashed. Most of us get "feelings" every day without giving it a second thought. It may be something as simple as thinking of someone right before they ring your phone. Most times we take these "feelings" for granted. But just imagine what we can do if we pay attention, focus and learn to increase the ability to use our psychic senses to warn us of impending danger, make better choices in our lives and communicate with those on the other side. After all, before we were born into this physical realm, we were connected to the spirit plane. The ability to connect with spirits is just remembering your native language. I simply approach it as a natural ability, a part of who I am-part of who we all are.

I am like many of you, going through my day, picking up kids from school, working, making dinner, doing laundry, all the regular activities that make up our daily lives. The only difference is, I have made the conscious choice to embrace my original language and continue to communicate with those existing in the realm from which

I came.

There is a growing fascination with the idea of communicating with spirits. Many TV shows regarding this phenomena, have become quite popular as there is an increase in curiosity about psychic phenomena and the idea that spirits still dwell in this place and can share information with us. Whether approached as a scientific or metaphysical process, the public appears to be clamoring for more information. Armed with cameras and tape recorders, even the most timid novice can be found staking out graveyards in search of the elusive ghostly manifestation. I have experienced malevolent entities staking claim to abandoned buildings, old hotels and invading cozy homes. With the ability to communicate with these spirits I discover why they are lingering, and help them move on, letting go of their earthly drama, and abandoning the people they have chosen to haunt. Whether they are lingering due to unfinished business or staying behind out of confusion or other reasons, it is interesting to explore. Many people fear the presence of spirits around them, especially in their living space. Having the ability to tell them the history and story of these paranormal manifestations helps assuage their fear and offers them answers and peace.

Trans-medium work or channeling is not something for the uninitiated. It is extremely intense. It requires a high level of connection to Spirit, a deep understanding of boundaries, protection and trust in higher self in order to allow another energy being to take over the physical self. It can be exhausting, as it requires a certain amount of controlled and focused energy to maintain the connection. Each spirit vibrates at its own frequency.

Dialing into a specific energy source and maintaining it, is tantamount to the process. There is always the danger of negative entities entering ones body and therefore a medium, which is what I am called, must be well equipped to handle those incidents to avoid risk to themselves and others. I have used this ability to solve crime cases, give messages to loved ones needing solace, and to remove wayward and sometimes negative spirits from homes, and various other locations.

This book uncovers the spirits who linger on Mackinac Island, describes who they were in life and why they remain, not ready to go home, and recounts the personal stories they wish to share with us.

As a psychic medium and clairvoyant I have spent twenty years delving into the supernatural realm. Spirits communicate through me, allowing connection with things far greater than ourselves. I am able to raise my vibrational level to meet the energy of those on the other side, creating a bridge for communication. Through these abilities I offer assistance to those seeking comfort in the knowledge that their loved ones are content and at peace on the other side.

Working with law enforcement officials, the voices of victims' speak through me, aiding in the discovery of their remains, and bringing closure to families devastated by loss of a loved one.

My psychic experiences at Mackinac Island, along with its legends and folklore, provide a rare glimpse into its unusual history, as well as the phenomena going on today. As one of the most paranormally active places in the United States, I offer you the opportunity to enter this land rich in history, filled with spiritual energy, and discover what truly lies on the other side. You can experience these phenomena, if only you knew where and how to look.

As a guide, this book is an invaluable tool to explore the island and its ghostly phenomena. For those interested in the paranormal, it offers an opportunity to become more aware of the ghostly plane, to hear the history and stories of the spirits that remain on the island. It is my hope to awaken your curiosity and help you venture beyond the mundane and travel past the limits we put on this human reality to discover a new and exciting way to look at the world around us.

For those seeking these experiences, Mists of Mackinac shares the beautiful Native American Lore, legends of old, and offers you a glimpse of the many paranormal phenomena present in this special place. Read on and enjoy this one of a kind experience.

Chapter 1

GHOSTS AMONG US

OST PEOPLE WHO SAY THEY want to see a ghost will run away screaming, at the sight of anything "unworldly". Whether it is a positive or negative entity, making a spirit connection evokes a variety of emotions. For paranormal investigators it is akin to finding the Holy Grail! Experiencing ghostly phenomena often involves all the senses. I have been grabbed by the throat by an angry entity and tossed to the ground, like a rag doll. I can attest that ghostly fingers do leave a mark. I have felt the icy chill of an entity entering my body, and watched as it moved my arms and legs and its voice came out of my mouth. I have been photographed with unearthly arms reaching out of my chest, as they tried to make their presence known. I have felt both the love and hate of disembodied entities, locked here on this plane. I have worked with clients who have been possessed by spirits, and witnessed a malevolent entity carving words in a woman's' back in answer to questions. Spirits are capable of doing many things, and it is wise to remember that.

Paranormal Investigations offer a chance to explore the unknown and communicate with beings hidden and silent to the majority of our earthly population. There are many different forms and reasons for ghostly activity. However it usually takes place on a higher vibration and therefore most people are not aware these beings are among us. Take for example a hummingbird. Upon first glance it appears this tiny creature is frozen midair, as their wings move at such a high rate of speed, the human eye does not see them, unless it is focuses intently. This is similar with a ghost or spirit, when we take the time to learn to focus our vibrational energy; to raise it higher, we increase our likelihood of making contact.

There are various types of ghosts. A sentient thinking ghost is the spirit of a deceased person. It could be a friend, relative, a stranger or historical figure. This was once a being on this plane. They have a history. They had a life, a job, a purpose. Their consciousness may be still be living out their human drama. Many times they believe they must continue their earthly purpose, complete a task, or may have a story to tell, or a job to do. At times they may feel the need to enlist the living in some type of help for situations or occurrences that are in reality a mere memory of their former life on this earth. They are re-living certain events in their life. These events appear to them in a continuous fashion, over and over again. They repeat behavior and situations never seeing the end result or conclusions in their lives. Usually these were events that they deemed important during their life. Other times they may be still caught up in their human drama and seeking help for some long ago situation or event. Usually they are unaware they could move on by just acknowledging the Light above, as all they really need do is allow themselves to see it, as it has been there all along, and follow it home. These types of spirits want to make themselves known,

Joan StJohn

to tell their story or to elicit help, and will make efforts to interact with those around them sensitive enough to connect.

This type of ghost is self-aware and intelligent, and capable of interacting with people through manifesting visibly, being heard audibly or telepathically, and even capable of touching the living. They also have the capability of manufacturing odors, such as perfume, cigarette or food smells, and moving objects, I have also seen them interfere with electrical and electronic objects. Such as turning on the TV, a light or interfering with a computer.

A sentient ghost is also capable of emotions. Just like a live person they can show anger, jealousy, rage, fear, happiness or sadness. An encounter with a sentient ghost can range from pleasant to horrific depending on the circumstance and emotional state of the ghost, and the actions of those attempting to communicate with it. In general they show themselves because they have a need, a want or are confused about their circumstances. Most people do not respond well to taunting or harassment, the same goes for spirits. They should be treated with respect as you would any human being, as they have feelings just like you.

A spirit may choose one person in the home to connect with, and quite often can enter a home attached to a piece of furniture or other item. It is the only type of spirit, except angelic or demonic beings, that can manifest interactive communication.

An example of this would be a ghost knocking on a table or moving of a pendulum, to a yes or no question, or the stopping and starting of clocks, turning on a radio, faucet television or other electrical appliance. Voice

20

recorders can capture their voices as well. These spirits seek ways to show their presence. My experiences with these types of spirits indicate they remember much of their former earthbound life and retain their personality traits, both positive and negative. They are capable of feeling emotions and during mediumship sessions I have found them capable of coming to conclusions regarding their situation, and having the ability to make decisions such as forgiving those that they feel have hurt them and to go forward into the Light. They are just like you and me; they seek answers to their questions. I choose to call this type of entity a spirit not a ghost as they are on a higher vibrational level then many of the other types of ghosts we will discuss below. This is a person who simply no longer resides in a body.

The most common of these spirits is what I will refer to as a familial spirit because they are intimately familiar to the person seeing them. This would be a loved one that appears immediately after death. At the time of their death this type of spirit will come to a family member, usually just once, in order to comfort them, say goodbye or let the grieving person know they are ok. Many times this familial spirit will appear in the dream of a loved one, making it easier for the family member to acknowledge them without fearing a full manifestation being presented before them. As I said before, a full manifestation of a spirit at the end of ones bed in the middle of the night is not always received well.

These sightings are the most difficult to confirm as they usually only manifest once and then the spirit moves on, content with the knowledge they have let their loved ones know that they are fine on the other side, and there is no need for worry. At times the appearance is to let the living family member know they have died. Many clients have shared with me they knew the exact moment their loved one passed, either because their loved one appeared to them, or due to a dream where the loved one showed them they were ok, and in some cases clients have heard their loved one whisper goodbye, and upon confirming the time, realized it was right at the time of death.

Whereas the thought of seeing ones dead family member may seem frightening to some, it does bring an incredible amount of comfort and solace, to the living, and it helps with closure, as having the knowledge that a deceased love one has let them know they are ok, helps them to understand and acknowledge that we all go on after death. The familial spirit seems to have a specific agenda connected to their communication and once that has been fulfilled they leave this plane and move on.

The second type of interactive spirit is the historical spirit. Not necessarily the ghost of Abraham Lincoln, but historical to the place it is making an appearance. An example would be the prior owner of a home that continues to believe they live there. This spirit makes their present known by continuing an activity as they did in life, such as closing windows and doors, or turning off the lights when they deem it is time for bed. They can also be attached to a physical object; a car, a piece of furniture as well as a house. They are consistent to a particular place and are considerably easier to document because of their longevity and predictability of being seen by others in the same locale. At the South Lyon Hotel, for instance, there lurks a spirit that manifests in the upper floor of the building and has been seen by several people in the restroom. At times when there is no one sitting at the bar, the smell of cigar smoke can be quite distinct. These are examples of a historical manifestation. Researching the building it was discovered that a man died in a fire, and his spirit manifests in this building, where he shows himself every now and then to unsuspecting women washing their hands in the ladies room. He has been known to grab a person by the shoulder leaving a hand shape type bruise. Perhaps you too may see him if you look in the mirror as you stand by the sink.

The third type of sentient spirit is considered 'anonymous'. It is unknown to both the witnesses and the place where it appears. It can be likened to a confused traveler that happened upon the location where they are appearing, many times not knowing where they are or why they are there and have no connection to the place or the people at that locale. Sometimes it appears they simply fell through a portal or doorway in that specific location and whereas they are not so thrilled to be there, they do not know what else to do, or how to leave. Yes, there are doorways to the other side all around us. Places where the division of this plane and the next are not so ridged and separate. Places where there are open windows instead of walls, which makes it easy for spirits to come through and enter our world. Such entities can be among the most difficult to interact with, for unlike the familial—who are here to comfort the grieving—or the historical—who consider themselves still a part of their environment, the anonymous frequently appear to be angry, frightened or confused, and often afraid of the living as the living are of them. While still capable of being documented and studied, they tend to be in a confused state and sometimes disoriented as they are unaware of their plight, and are seemingly in the wrong place and time. Due to this they do not generally make as good 'test cases' as others.

These three sub-categories can be interchangeable as for example a familial spirit may be someone else's historic or another person's anonymous depending upon the relationship of the witness to the manifestation. These terms have little to do with the reality of the situation, but are more to identify the spirit to the observer. Sentient spirits wish to engage someone into their earthly situation, not realizing their bond to the earth and all its earthly dramas and situations are over.

Janice, was 42, when we met, she was conducting regular automatic writing sessions to improve her spirit communication skills. She began to receive disturbing messages from a woman who claimed to have been murdered. This spirit continued to insist Janice go to a remote wooded area, the location of which she showed her through the automatic writing. When Janice refused to go, she began to awaken in the middle of the night to soft sobbing sounds. She also started experiencing dreams where this spirit was begging her for help. At one point she received a message indicating the spirit wanted her to dig up her body and remove a ruby ring from her finger as payment for helping to resolve her murder. Drawn to go digging, but not wanting to go alone, and with growing alarmed over the nightly sobbing noise that began to increase in volume, she contacted me for help.

My first instruction to Janice was to put down the shovel. While exhuming human remains, and solving a possible murder mystery would be exciting for some, it can also lead to pesky questions by police, as to how you knew there was a body buried in some remote wooded location inaccessible and out of view to most of the population. There is also what I like to refer to as the "creepy" factor of unearthing a desiccating corpse, as well as the distasteful concept of removing jewelry items off a dead body. Not wanting to be party to a potential grave robbing adventure and being mindful of another situation where the murderer lived in close proximity to the dump site, and therefore in full view of whomever was lurking about. I convinced Janice to conduct the session in my office.

Psychics have to be aware that sharing knowledge about a crime can make you a suspect, which can be unpleasant, time consuming and costly. I am usually contacted by family members, who I then ask to give my number to the detective in charge of the case, who then calls me. I very rarely will give family members information directly as I am very aware of the sensitive nature of the information and feel law enforcement officers are best able to handle the information that I garner.

I continue to locate murder victims for law enforcement agencies but the idea of stomping through the woods, shovels in hand, without law enforcement along, is not safe or prudent. If nothing else it will most likely contaminate a crime scene and interfere with any further police investigation and evidence gathering. In the worst case, the perpetrator may see you, and that would put your own life in danger. I strongly suggest if the opportunity ever arises, the reader would keep that in mind.

I do not need to physically go to the crime scene, as I am able to see it through remote viewing, which is the ability to psychically see a physical location without having to actually be there. I am able to draw accurate maps of the area, as well as see landmarks and other identifiers. Many times the victim will "walk" me through the scene and I can see it out of their eyes. It is important to understand that solving crimes is under the jurisdiction of law enforcement agencies. I only assist when asked, and think of myself as a guest. I do this work with the provision that my name not be used or associated with the case and if added, only as a community volunteer. I respect the position of law enforcement officials, they work hard at what they do, and they put their lives on the line to protect the citizens of our cities. I prefer to assist quietly in the background, as solving crimes is their job, not mine. I feel blessed to be able to offer concrete assistance, and thankful to have the ability to help family members glean some closure from the loss of their loved ones.

I agreed to conduct an interview with Janice, and then channel the spirit to discover why it was haunting her home and her dreams.

When conducting a paranormal investigation, it is important to interview the individual that is experiencing the phenomena. Weeding out the psychotic and mentally ill, will save you time, and energy. They are out there, believe me, and once they find out you do paranormal investigations they will call you…numerous times… as they want some other reasons besides mental illness for what they are experiencing. So please remember not all "voices" that people tell you they hear, are from spirits. Part of your initial interview is to ask if the client is on any type of drugs, psychotropic or otherwise. Also, ask if they are bipolar or have any other mental illness, or have been committed to a mental hospital. Please be professional and compassionate about it.

I was contacted by a man who was convinced there was a spirit communicating to him through his car, instructing him to do things that were counterproductive to his highest good and physically dangerous. He explained the voices were telling him to sleep and eat in his car, instead of his apartment, and when he was driving would tell him to drive his car into a tree at high speed. Through my interview questions I discovered he was under psychiatric care, and had been diagnosed with schizophrenia, was currently taking large doses of medication, had tried to commit suicide and had been committed several times against his will to a psychiatric facility.

I psychically ascertained there was no spiritual presence involved in this situation, and it was easy to see this was a person at risk.

There are many unscrupulous people, who would take advantage of someone such as this, as this client desperately wanted to believe the voices were caused by an external source, rather than admit they were a manifestation of his illness. A health scan revealed his aura was extremely fractured, another indication for me, of mental illness. As a medical intuitive, illnesses show themselves to me in certain ways. In this case I found it easy to see he was mentally unstable. He gladly gave me permission to speak with his psychiatrist, as I felt it was in the clients' best interest to elicit his doctors' support before conducting a reading. At my insistence, the psychiatrist agreed that it would be in the clients' best interest to have the reading with the psychiatrist present, in order to deal with anything that may come out in the reading, and to have the support necessary when telling the client this was not a spiritual matter, but a psychological one. The session went smoothly, and the psychiatrist was able to guide him through the information that was presented to him in the reading, assisting him with the reality that it was his illness that was creating these "voices". His medication was increased and he has not heard the voices, or has not tried to commit suicide since. Realizing that sometimes the answer is not psychic in nature is as important as being able to identify a psychic problem.

When interviewing look over the surroundings carefully. One woman insisted there were ghosts in her pantry. Upon arriving at her home, the filth was intolerable, which included an enormous amount of mice feces in the pantry…mystery solved….

Janice turned out to be a viable client, rooted in reality. Upon channeling the spirit in this case, I discovered that Melinda, as she called herself, was from the mid 1800's and indicated she was murdered by her husband. This spirit was caught in a time and space that no longer existed. There was no one to punish for her death, nothing current about her situation. It was a looped memory that continued long after all involved had died. The desire for Melinda to offer payment was also indicative of her being caught in her human drama. Looking psychically at the wooded area Janice had been drawn to, I could see that the earth had not been disturbed in a long time.

Though the spirit was in a seemingly distressed state, it was only because she was unaware that she had the option to leave, by connecting to the Light. Her human drama continued, as she was not aware it no longer of any consequence. I was able to successfully transmit her spirit to the other side, and help her move on. Whether Janice attempted to dig up the corpse, to find the ring, I do not know, as once the spirit experiences release from the drama and trauma suffered on this plane, my job was complete.

Another interesting case was that of Tara, who at age fourteen was being haunted by the spirit of an older man named James. He hovered in her bedroom, filling her dreams with warnings. He appeared agitated which frightened her. I was contacted by her mother to help get rid of this unwanted houseguest. I discovered through channeling that this particular spirit was attached to a table my client had inherited from her mother. When I explained this to her, the client remembered Tara would see the same ghostly man at her grandmothers' home, when her grandmother had the table.

Upon further communication with this spirit I discovered that he had been a servant in a household where a young girl had drowned. He felt responsible and substituted Tara for the girl, and continued to try to warn her. He came to her in dreams, as well as a shadow in her room. He was so consumed with feelings of obligation and dread, that his intense insistence with Tara, and the strong energy he emitted, frightened her. The entity concentrated in her room. I observed her cat, Molly would not enter her bedroom, but sat by the doorway hissing. In my work with the spirit I was able to detach him from his earth bound connections and feelings, and help him move onward, no longer lingering in the drama of his earthly past. Tara no longer felt his ominous presence and I observed the cat, enter her room, and from what I last heard from Tara, Molly happily resides there.

Next we have what is basically a place memory, or reoccurring ghost: This type, also once human, seems to be stuck in one specific time and place. They appear to be unaware of current events, but view their environment from the perspective of when they lived. They repeat an activity that may have been important in life. Most paranormal investigators believe these types of spirits cannot communicate however in my experience as a medium I know differently. I call these types of spirits "stuck". Most times they do not realize they no longer have to continue with their earthly activity and are happy to move on, once I communicate this to them and assist in guiding them home. This type of spirit is different from an "imprint" memory which we will discuss later.

Terri, an accountant with her own firm, contacted me with a concern regarding the windows in her office. She indicated they would shut unassisted as if suddenly dropped closed, yet would stick terribly when she or her coworkers tried to open or shut them. The building was built in the early 1900's, originally as a large home, and later converted to office space. Every day at 4pm the windows would start to close one by one. These episodes were causing quite the disturbance in her office, as workers were beginning to feel frightened by this constant ghostly activity. They could hear the windows bang shut, room by room, as if someone was slamming them, followed by loud footsteps, as if someone was walking down the hall, entering each room and shutting the windows. Most of the employees had seen the windows drop as if an invisible force had slammed them down and several had quit after witnessing these supernatural occurrences.

Terri consulted me regarding the problem and I discovered through my channeling session that these events were the manifestation of a spirit who identified himself by the name, Louis. He was once the caretaker of this building, when it was a home, and one of his jobs was to shut the windows. Unfortunately for the current occupants, Louis, the ever devoted employee, continued to do his job, despite the fact that he was no longer alive. He saw the building as it existed in his time, and was annoyed that the windows continued to remain open. He was not cognizant of the people in the building, or who was opening the windows. All he was aware of was that the windows were open and it was his job to close them before the night air could enter the house. He told me in detail how the "night air" was the culprit for causing illness, and closing the windows protected the children, and therefore the windows had to be shut before sundown.

One could imagine how frustrating it could have been for poor Louis, so emotionally connected to doing his earthly job, and never understanding why the windows would not remain shut, creating a never ending job in a continuous cycle. I helped Louis shift his consciousness and he was finally able to stop closing windows, move toward the Light, and finally retire from his endless job. The office workers now have to shut the windows themselves which they are happy to do. However they did put up a plaque honoring Louis as the employee with the longest work record.

These types of spirits live in more of an emotional state than a state of being. It is as if the tape of the event plays continuously without conclusion. The spirit is locked in performing this act because their emotions are so tied to it, that they do not make the effort to look up and move on. On some level they see no other reality but the action they continue to perform. Most cases they do not know they have the ability to stop it. They feel emotional attached or obligated to continue. It is seen as an obsessive act. As if the spirit is locked in performing the action because their emotions are so tied to it, that they do not make the effort to look up and move on.

Another situation was brought to me by Mary, a mom of a five year old boy. She and her family had recently moved into a home that was built in the 1800's and were in the process of refurbishing it.

Mary's son, Ethan had always slept with the lights out, however each morning Mary would discover the light on in his bedroom closet. This went on for several weeks, until she asked her son about it. What he told her chilled her to the bone. "Mommy," he said, "Don't you remember? You come into my room every night, sing me a song and turn on the closet light." Mary, fearing for her son's safety, contacted me.

During the channeling session I discovered the spirit was a nanny named Bridget who along with her young charge died in out outbreak of typhoid. Historical records confirmed this. It was her duty to care for a young boy, and even in death she continued her job, not realizing that both she and the young boy she cared for were both long dead.

I was able to help Bridget realize her presence was unnecessary, on this plane, and she went lovingly to the light. Ethan still sings the lullaby she taught him, Irish brogue and all.

With both these occurrences there are similar manifestations. Sound, smell, moving objects, visions, tastes, changes in temperature, and manifestations within the person experiencing this event.

There is also another paranormal event called an

energy imprint. This is where the space or land seemingly has absorbed the energy of the event and plays it as a looped version of a movie clip. For example the final scream of a miner in a shaft before he dies or the ghostly mother crying for her child. The energy of the scream or cry is captured and imprinted into the physical place and can be heard repeatedly. There is no active ghost or spirit here. The event has simply been recorded. This can be likened to creating a vase on a potters' wheel. When using a stylus to make lines in the clay as it is turning on the wheel, it records, like a record, the voices and noises in the room at the time. Even after firing in a kiln, these sounds can be heard. These types of "recorded" events are most commonly in place of trauma. For instance, the sounds of children screaming on the site of a school fire, where many died. It can be very chilling to experience, but as it is not an active spirit, there is no ability for communication. It is merely an imprint of a past occurrence, and can be whipped clean easily with certain cleansing rituals.

Not all ghostly manifestations are animate in nature. Inanimate objects such as the sightings of "ghost ships" and "phantom aircraft" have been reported regularly and remain amongst the most inexplicable ghostly presence. As is commonly understood these objects do not have a consciousness and were never alive in the sense of being human. The best way these types of apparitions can be described as "snap shots" or imprinted memories on a particular place. Like a prerecorded message that plays continually for all those with the ability to see them. They pose no threat and like their vocal counterpart, are just a memory energy imprint left upon the earth.

Animal spirit manifestations are quite common in

Native American tales and history. The animal totem is a very powerful presence in their culture and traditions. Many people disagree as to the ability of animals to possess the sentience necessary to be considered a conscious personality. However animals possess far more emotions than many people give them credit for. In my experience a family pet will make its presence known to the family that loved him, as the connection through love is extremely strong. An animal that senses love on this physical plane will continue to connect on the spiritual. There are many stories of a beloved pet walking the halls of the family home, or climbing upon the bed, as it did in life, to sleep with its master. There are many theories about this, as with everything else, and it is up to the reader to believe what they wish, as no one actually knows for sure. It is a matter of what someone has experienced and how they choose to define it. So whatever theory or explanation resonates with you is what you can choose to believe. I can only share my experiences to explain how I have come to my own beliefs, and hope that assists you in making your own determination.

In my experience it seems a natural progression to believe animals can come through the veil after death to be with those their loved, just like people do.

Toby was a rescued Australian Shepard who was very close to the family she lived with. A natural herder, she seemed to be most content when the entire family was in one room. It was common for her to walk through the house and herd the children into the living room. They delighted in her efforts, which appeared to please her even more. After she died, she could occasionally be seen standing in the hallway, as if waiting for the children to exit their bedrooms so she could "herd" them into the living room. Sometimes she could be seen standing by the front door, waiting for her family's return.

Another type of ghostly presence is that of the Celestials. They are distinguished from other spirits as they are not of human origin, nor have they ever manifested on earth in body form. Working from the premise that we, humans are not the only sentient beings in the universe, we can easily accept this concept. These beings include Angels, Spirit Guides, Master Souls, ancient intellectuals, as well as spirits from other planets or extraterrestrials, as they are common called. They appear to be inter-dimensional beings existing on another plane, but willing to teach and help us here in this place called Earth. These are the high vibrational spirits that often come to us in meditative states, when we are asking for guidance or when we are in need of help in emergency situations. They are frequently spiritual masters offering wisdom in human affairs. Additionally, celestials are extremely difficult to document, as they normally interact in more subtle and non-perceivable ways.

Spirit Guides are specific to individual people. They can be viewed as a tutor assigned to us in life to help us increase our vibrational energy while we are here. We may have more than one in our lifetime or consecutively, depending upon our needs. For instance in my work I have one guide that comes through when I am conducting a health scan, assisting me to see ailments and dis-ease in the physical body. He guides me through the systems of the body as if it were a map, enabling me to identify health issues. There is another guide I refer to as my "detective", who works me during remote viewing sessions, which comes in very handy when locating murder victims and missing persons. I work consistently with five to six different guides or entities in my work, depending on what my needs are and how I choose to approach a situation.

Spirit Guides in general tend to work in the background, and more times than not, allow us to think the ideas and help they provide come from our higher self, which is part of how they teach us to trust our inner voice. They are less likely to manifest outside ourselves as that would defeat the purpose they have of helping us trust more in ourselves than outside sources. Their goal is to teach us to move forward in this life with strength and self-trust, and too look inward, not outward for answers. A guide is just that, an entity that helps to illuminate a pathway, it is up to the individual to choose to follow its light.

Now we come to the phenomena known as Poltergeists, which has been surrounded by controversy and speculation. A Poltergeist differs from what is normally thought of as a ghost. Ghosts are usually considered to be, the spirits of dead people. The word "poltergeist" came from the German word "poltern," which means to "rumble", "bluster", or "jangle", and "geist," which means "spirit." Usually described as an invisible force, the nature of poltergeists has long been, and still is, a subject of debate within paranormal circles. Poltergeists are a different sort of manifestation that has little to do with the typical type of haunting. These manifestations seem to be able to interact with the material world, sometimes with malevolent force.

In past centuries, poltergeist activity was attributed to demons and witches. The progress of paranormal science and parapsychology during the 20th century gave rise to a new concept about the nature of poltergeists.

Physicist Vladistav Bukreev[3], studied the unknown, including poltergeist, UFO's, magnetic fields and such. He investigated the poltergeist activity centering on an English family living in Enfield, a northern area of London during the time period of 1977—1978.

Bukreev tells of "showers of stones and bricks" as well as house windows being smashed, and objects flying about the house. He indicated that the family suffered what appeared to be "bite or claw marks on their bodies" and the two young girls of the family were said to be "lifted up into the air and moved around with no apparent support." It seems after almost a year of this torment with no reprieve in sight, the family fled the home.

This study which came to be referred to as "The Enfield Phenomenon" gave rise to much speculation among the scientific paranormal community at the time, regarding the link between the presence of children, especially pubescent girls, and the manifested signs of poltergeist activity. Researchers began to interpret poltergeist as an unusual display of sexually-charged mental tension. It was regarded at that time, as a safety valve for venting intense energy.[4]

According to Bukreev, The basis of a "noisy spirit" can be built of energy, physical, chemical, biological, and mental components. He believed that nature programmed the poltergeist into every human being and common nervous breakdowns and explosive mental states are the poltergeist manifestations of a soul that is deeply distressed by grievous events of the outside world.[5]

Scientists Pierro Brovetto, Vera Maxia from the Instituto Fisica Superiore in Cagliara, Italy[6] noted that poltergeist activities have been reported across different cultures worldwide, and they too felt this type of activity was somehow tied to the proximity of pubescent young women. They hypothesized that the changes of the brain that occur at puberty involve "fluctuations in electron activity and that in these cases it can create disturbances up to a few meters around the outside of the brain, similar to the quantum mechanical fluctuations that physicists believe occur in the vacuum, in which "virtual" particle and antiparticle pairs pop up for a fleeting moment before they annihilate each other and disappear again. These extra fluctuations triggered by the pubescent brain would substantially enhance the presence of the virtual particles surrounding the person, slowly increasing the pressure of air around them, moving objects and even sending them hurling across the room."[7]

"A decrease in entropy (creation of order) in the brain of pubescent people throws a greater amount of entropy (disorder) into the brain environment, which, in exceptional cases, originates poltergeist disturbances, in practice, poltergeist is interpreted as a by-product of an entropy increase in vacuum. This interpretation is based on two sound achievements of the past century physics, that is, quantum electrodynamics of vacuum and nonequilibrium thermodynamics."[8]

Separate studies done by parapsychologists Nandor Fodor[9], Alan Gauld[10] and A. D. (Tony)Cornell[11], and William Roll also traced poltergeist existence and activity not in paranormal entities but in humans. According to their theories on the human-poltergeist connection, the forces usually ascribed to poltergeists are powerful emotional and mental triggers in the human psyche. These theories have their foundations on the idea that poltergeist activity usually occurs in places which have seen much violence and suffering or around persons who are experiencing deep emotional turmoil. William Roll[12] named the phenomenon as "recurrent spontaneous psychokinesis" or RSPK. This refers to the expression of intense emotion like hostility, anger, and sexual tension from a human agent who causes inexplicable physical manifestations such as levitation, items being thrown across the room and unexplained combustion. The agent is usually oblivious to the fact the he or she caused the disturbance because it is the subconscious mind which found a way to release any repressed emotion through psychokinesis.[13]

On the other hand, poltergeist activity without the presence of an agent is attributed to the remnants of intense emotions in a particular locale, a phenomenon similar to how a place gives one "the creeps" without any apparent reason. In this case, poltergeist activity is simply seen an outward manifestation of human emotion. It is perfectly controllable as long as the agent expresses pent-up feelings, hence, lessening chances of subconscious "poltergeist" activity.

Then again, many believe that a poltergeist is an elemental, akin to what would be called the "Fae". A childlike spirit that is easily upset or angered. Or as a combination of a malicious or mischievous spirit fueled or energized by the angry or turbulent energy of the people around it.

Despite the differing opinions about the nature of poltergeists, one thing is definite—they do exist. Whether poltergeists are paranormal entities or psychic forces, they continue to be seen and studied as interesting phenomena, whether as a manifestation of the torment of the soul, or an outside force to be reckoned with, is yours to decide.

I do not believe poltergeist is solely manufactured in the brain of pubescent girls, as if that were so, every middle school would be inundated with such activity. Whereas I believe we have much untapped potential in our brains, there has to be a correlation between our subconscious abilities and the energy of spirits in the universe, where the perfect pairing of both results in such activity.

There are ways to get rid of poltergeist activity, but as there is much speculation as to the cause, it is best left for those with experience in such matters as it takes a certain skill-set, knowledge and ability to become aware of the particular circumstances leading to understanding of the energy resonance of things and events.

Examining the Evidence

It is widely accepted by many cultures that something remains after the body dies. It is often referred to as our "soul" or "spirit", and considered our ethereal body, or the very essence of life itself. It is commonly believed that the spirit "goes on" after death, and is no longer on the same plane of existence as those who are living. Referred to as heaven, nirvana, "the other side", whether it is a vision of sitting on a cloud, or being in a beautiful lush green garden, everyone has a different view of what to expect. But for a moment imagine that this is not true. Imagine that the dead exist right here with us, on the same plane, but vibrate at a higher frequency unseen by the naked eye.

We have heard stories of ghostly apparitions and some of you may have even seen things that don't seem to belong in our present state of reality. Although they may not be of the flesh, or exist as we do in this physical plane, they are amongst us. It is some type of evidence of these spirits existence we seek when conducting a paranormal investigation. But not all photos, sound bites, and videos are authentic. The issue of authenticity with any evidence can dampen even the most enthusiastic ghost hunter. It takes a keen eye and experience in this area to determine whether a video, voice recording, or photo is actually evidence and not explainable as something else, as many end up being. Whether a water droplet on the lens, a shadow of another person moving into your filming area, or noise from the outside that is being picked up on the recording, that are just simply ordinary earthly occurrences. People do many unconscious things, such as tapping a foot, humming, or moving about the room where the cameras are situated without realizing they are altering the outcome of their investigation. But when evidence gathered is beyond a reasonable doubt, and there is no other explanation for it, no matter how you try to duplicate or debunk it, then you have hit pay dirt and it is an amazing feeling to have something like that in hand.

Authentic evidence however uncommon, is what we seek when ghost hunting. There are many ways to garner this evidence, one way is with the help of a psychic medium.

There is a division within the ghost hunting community as to whether psychic mediums have a place in the science of documenting ghostly activity. Some feel it takes away from the credibility of their work as "scientists". Others feel it enhances the ability to gain valuable spirit evidence through direct communication. The groups that acknowledge a psychic mediums' place on their team use both technical tools that measure heat, movement, record voice and images and the skills a medium has to offer, which include direct communication with the spirit.

Ghost hunting is basically a "set up the equipment and wait" process, which can mean long hours of sitting in the dark waiting for something to happen. In most cases the evidence is seen later when reviewing the many hours of video or voice recordings. A psychic medium offers an additional way to gather evidence by being able to sense the presence and location of a spirit as well as directly communicate with them. Some have the added ability to be able to draw them out to increase the opportunity to be captured by the technical equipment in the form of photographs and sound.

My abilities as a psychic medium, allows me to communicate with spirits to discover why they are present, what they need, and why they have not gone on. This includes pinpointing their location, and at times what I am hearing as their reply, will be captured on the tape recorder even though others in the room do not hear it.

Here is an example of how a spirit can manifest on our vibrational plane. In this photo I am at the scene of a paranormal investigation where reports were made concerning the presence of negative spirit activity. During my channeling session this photo was taken.

I am standing on the left, and there is a black shadowy apparition behind me. I am standing in the doorway of a long hallway eliminating the possibility of it being a mere shadowy reflection on the wall. Also, you can clearly see an arm and hand of mist jutting out from me going across one of the individuals on the right side of the photo. After seeing this photo, we tried to replicate it by retaking the photograph but no matter what angle we took the shot at, we were not able to duplicate both the shadow or the mist like arm protruding from me. During the channeling session I could feel the entity entering my body in the form of an icy cold temperature as well. There are ghosts among us, now it is a matter of whether or not you wish to see for yourself.

The idea of ghosts is not new to Mackinac Island. Here, folklore tales and ghost stories are passed from one generation to the next. These stories continue to draw the attention of those coming to the island. But how do you know what is, and what isn't a ghostly manifestation?

Experiencing paranormal phenomena differs for each individual. Some see it with their physical eyes; some with their psychic eye. It can be a feeling, such as of being watched or the the sensation of having the hair on the back of your arms raised by what may feel like an electrical force. People who are clairaudient, will hear voices, as if the spirit is speaking loudly in the room. It is also common to feel a change in temperature, a wave of nausea, or a sudden loss of equilibrium as if the room itself is shifting. Experiencing actual physical changes within the body, is quite common when presented with a spiritual presence. Most people do not recognize it for what it is. But paying close attention to changes in temperature, fluxuations in feelings, and subtle changes within ones own body works as a wonderful meter to identify the presence of spirit activity around you. There are many ways spirits make themselves known. It differs with each person. What you may feel, see or hear is very personal in nature. Be open to all the subtlties and whatever the experience may be for you.

Avoid the pitfall of trying to create boundaries and limitations around what you may think is or is not classified as a true ghostly encounter. The biggest problem one can create when ghost hunting is to approached it with preconcieved ideas, expectations, or judgements. When you second guess yourself you create a situation where you doubt the validity of the experience and negate the possibility that the encounter was real. Being open to the experience whatever it may be for you, is an important step in developing the ability to increase your awareness of spirit presence.

I hope the experiences I have shared with you in this book help to increase your awareness, open up your imagination, and assist you in seeing the world as a bigger place than before.

Now that you are ready, we shall enter the mystical world of Mackinac Island!

Chapter 2

THE INNS AT MACKINAC ISLAND

A S THE SUGARY SMELL OF fudge combined with the pungent odor of horses, assailed my nostrils, I was aware of a distinct energy shift. The island shimmered, as a heat wave on hot asphalt. I had to be careful disembarking the ferry, for the land did not appear firm under my feet. Amazingly, beneath the cacophony of crowded streets, people talking and the noises of the carriages as they squeaked and croaked under the weight of passengers, I felt a sense of tranquility. I can almost see the Ojibwa sentries at their posts. The sense of men waiting for ships to arrive, of children whooping with delight as they spot the canoes on the horizon, and of women sending out silent prayers of thanks as the great water delivers their husbands home safely.

An inner peace prevails within this island. Remnants from the original occupants who knew this was a special place. Red Sun, my spirit guide tells me that this place is sacred, and all who come to live here must realize it also. It is obvious to me that the present inhabitants have listened to this message as eighty percent of Mackinac Island is dedicated as state park land and those that dwell here have been faithful to the original inhabitants desire to protect this piece of earth, this Great Turtle, considered being the first piece of land created on this earth, the Ojibwa Eden.

I am here on Mackinac Island at the urging of my friend and paranormal investigator Robb Kaczor, to investigate for ourselves the paranormal activities attributed to this island and attempt to communicate with the otherworldly beings that reside here.

And so it begins.

Pine Cottage

First on my list to explore was Pine Cottage. My experience there proved it to be one of the most paranormally active locations I found on Mackinac Island. Folklore tales report several entities seemingly active in the Pine Cottage. In researching the stories of ghosts that are said to inhabit Pine Cottage, I have learned they have simply been named, "the creature," "the man," "the woman," and "the little girl."

Upon our arrival, we made our way past the crowded docks and Main Street overflowing with horse drawn carriages, bicyclers and busy tourists, and headed to the Pine Cottage which is located about halfway along Bogan's Lane, two blocks away from the boat docks on Lake Huron. The walk was pleasant, a kaleidoscope of flowers dotted the landscape, the sun dancing atop the waves, cruising boats, big and small, standing tall, a line of swaying soldiers at the dock. This is an idyllic place where the pace slows naturally for tourists as they conform unconsciously to the cadence of the Island.

Pine Cottage looms before us, a sedate respite for the weary traveler, nestled behind an ostentatiously painted towering Victorian that rivals only the Remington House for its architecturally bastardized add-ons, and across from The Chateau Lorraine, which seemingly springs to life before my "psychic" eye…but more about Chateau Lorraine later.

My attention is immediately riveted to the attic and I glimpsed the shadowy figure of a young girl in the right hand window who stares out longingly, filling me with the sense that she has a need that has not yet been fulfilled. As I contemplated the wave of sadness that she projected, she vanishes as suddenly as she had appeared. At this point I knew I would be in for an interesting time!

The Pine Cottage is said to contain forty-two rooms within its three floors. As well as being a popular bed & breakfast on the island, has a reputation for its ghostly visitors. A popular story is the tale of the ghostly woman. Legend has it that a woman who lived in the house was brutally murdered in 1942. Stories include seeing a woman in 1940's garb standing near the Pine Cottage looking up at the second story windows, as well as the sight of a shadowy figure of a woman appearing on the second floor hallway.

Could it be her ghost that still haunts this place?

Mackinac Island is perhaps one of Michigan's most scenic and visited spots. It lies off the north shore of the mainland peninsula and in the waters of Lake Huron.

49

During the summer months, it is packed with tourists and vacationers, but in the winter months frozen Lake Huron creates a resolute impasse.

A common tale includes Bob Hughey who came to Mackinac Island, opening a restaurant called Little Bob's. After World War II, he married and expanded his business, purchasing Pine Cottage in 1962. Legend has it that it was in the spring of that year when he realized he was sharing the house with "something" else. The strange sounds of footsteps and doors opening and closing began to be heard that could not be explained. Searches revealed no reasonable or earthly explanation. The story goes that things took a more frightening turn that year when Bob walked into a room on the first floor. Suddenly, from out of the closet, a woman rushed madly at him...more like through him, only to disappear out the window. As reported, his most frightened moment was when he realized she had only been visible from the waist up!

That was just the beginning. The strange sightings of many spirits continued, from men standing next to beds at night to a little girl that had been reported crying at the attic window. The little girl has been reported all over the house since then. Both staff members and visitors talked of hearing her footsteps and other strange sounds and items turning up missing. Even more disturbing having their bedcovers pulled off them in the middle of the night.

Another ghostly tale connected to the Pine Cottage is that of "The Creature". This apparition has been described as looking like a hunched man, horns protruding from his back, with eyes glowing red. It is said that after a heated argument with his wife, a previous owner went off to sleep in a different room. He then awoke in the middle of the night when the blankets had been pulled from his bed. He is said to have spotted the creature at the foot of his bed, staring at him, and at the shocking sight of it, made a hasty exit and returned to his spouse.

I have seen similar creature like apparitions. On a trip to the Catskill Mountains in NY, I stopped at a bed & breakfast in Shandelee. Ignoring the first red flag, that there were no other guests, I entered my designated room, and sat on the bed to assess my rather dingy surroundings. Feeling someone staring at me I glanced at the wooden bench in the corner of the room, and there smiling menacingly, sat four entities shoulder to shoulder, , leaning toward me with pointed, jagged teeth and glowing red eyes. Not a good sign by any stretch of the imagination. As I sensed the beings were well rooted in this building, and I was the intruder. Within two minutes I was out the door, looking for the nearest Holiday Inn.

Just because I am a psychic medium does not mean I welcome the idea of spending the night fending off evil entities, and it is not up to me to exorcise evil from every place I go to. Sometimes it is best to leave things alone, and move on, especially if outnumbered.

The story I found most interesting about the Pine Cottage was that of the tale of a little girl who it has been said appears at The Pine Cottage and across the street playing piano at the Chateau Lorraine, another bed and breakfast.

In researching this story, it is said that the young girl was left behind when her vacationing parents, ardent drinkers, returned home to Detroit without her. It is said that this young girl died soon after and has been seen weeping and on occasion heard to cry, "Mommy, I want to come home."

I found this tale hard to believe. Having children, myself, I know how difficult it is to get time to oneself, let alone leave them behind somewhere. I assumed at some point in time the parents would realize they had left her behind. If there was a delay in that action I was sure the staff would have had the mental acumen to contact local authorities, rather than merely take her in like a lost puppy. Putting my pragmatic self on hold and unable to resist this challenge, I entered the Pine Cottage.

Upon entering the building I felt my psychic antenna alerted. I could already sense the spirit activity within. The room was well appointed with lace curtains and Victorian era artifacts and beautifully crafted banisters, all welcoming to visitors. Yet there was activity brewing in these silent rooms. I began to psychically tune into this underlying energy. As I raised my vibration to communicate with the spirits I heard the name Sarah Jane Pitman, and the rest of the information came through as if I was reading from a book.

It was the early 1900's and Sarah was spending the month of August with her parents at the Pine Cottage. Long blonde hair rolled expertly in "Shirley Temple" style curls; a peach bow in her hair, complimenting the peach colored sash on her crisp white dress, Sarah was eight years old. Her parents were told she was in delicate health and a month on the island would do her good. Walks in the woods, relaxing by the lake did nothing to strengthen Sarah's' constitution. The fever came and Sarah died one morning from typhoid. Her mother, distraught and unable to cope with these events was hurried off the island by her husband, Sarah's stepfather. Sarah was secretly buried on the island. I saw her clearly standing in the right corner window, top floor of the Pine Cottage. Looking down, feeling incredibly sad and lost. There she waits her parents return, left behind, not as a living child but as a spirit seeking closure and wanting to go home.

My connection with Sarah was very strong. She was able to convey her feelings and desires easily. Her sadness washed over me, and I felt her longing. It is a common phenomenon for some spirits to stay behind, "stuck" in their earthly drama, thinking they have to wait for a human event to occur, in this case, the return of her parents, before they are willing to come to the realization that they can move on. Some would explain it as the spirit is not cognizant that they are dead, as they are viewing only the movie of their life during that moment in time, unaware that they have the ability to transcend the earthly drama. Since Sarah was buried on the island, a place she did not feel was home, she felt left behind. She was buried in secret to possibly avoid a typhoid scare that would have disrupted the economic wellbeing of the Island. Her only connection to the Island was of the Pine Cottage: she remains there waiting to go home. This is the girl I saw looking out of the attic window upon my arrival. Would finding her resting place release her? Not likely for unless she is ready to move on, she will choose to stay a permanent fixture at The Pine Cottage, greeting the unsuspecting guests and asking for her mother.

There was nothing to suggest that there were any negative entities in this place. Sarah seemed to be the only active spirit. Whether or not the stories are true that a murdered woman haunts The Pine Cottage is no longer evident by the present spirit activity and energy. If she ever existed, her spirit has already gone on.

"The creature," a non-human looking form, manifests due to absorption of the energy around it. Think of it as an empty glass. If overfilled with water, it spills onto the table, no longer contained in its receptacle. If someone comes into a space emitting negative or angry energy, it will be absorbed by the creature. The tale of the man is an example of this, as he was in a state of anger when entering this room, and no doubt fussing about the argument with his wife when his anger added to this pocket of negative energy, increasing it. The negative energy of this pocket is still evident in the building, though not harmful, can still be felt by those sensitive enough to recognize energy shifts.

There did seem to be a lot of spiritual "chatter" going on. As if someone was replaying a tape repeatedly. Sound bites of past activity are captured within the building as these events appear to continue. It felt homey and welcoming, like entering a room where everyone is eating breakfast and beckon you to join them. A pleasant place and I easily understand why so many people return to the Pine Cottage Bed & Breakfast, year after year.

THE CHATEAU LORRAINE

Across the street from the Pine Cottage, built in the 1880's, stands the Chateau Lorraine. It is said to be the site of a lone weeping girl, some reports indicate it is the same young girl that haunts the Pine Cottage. Other published works indicate it a place of sadness, death and sorrow. I did not find sorrow in this place. Nor was there the sense of fear or negative energy, which gave me a chuckle after reading such dramatic tales.

In researching its history, there is not much written about ghostly evidence at The Chateau Lorraine, except a report of a brief siting of the supposed weeping young girl.

As I stood in front of the building I was taken aback by the sudden sounds of the tinkering of piano keys, and voices in lively conversation reminiscent of moonshiners and gangsters hanging out at a speakeasy. I could see men sitting around a table, their side arms resting in their shoulder holsters casually tossed on the backs of their chairs, playing poker and drinking liquor. Tendrils of smoke swirling about their heads as they chewed on their cigars, concentrating on the playing cards they were dealt. The smell of the aromatic tobacco, as it curled out the opened window drew me closer. I heard their chatter and felt the sense that they were on vacation from their usual unlawful pursuits. The music from the piano, ladies laughter and men carousing affected a party atmosphere encompassing the entire Chateau Lorraine. I felt a twinge of disappointment when I walked through the door to find the room ghostly still and empty. I certainly would have enjoyed meeting these colorful characters.

My experience was a far cry from past stories fabricated to taunt the timid. The Chateau Lorraine maintains a festive energy that would offer a positive experience to any guest. Walk past the front window of the Chateau Lorraine, and see if you too can take a whiff of the cigars, or hear the tinkering of piano keys, and enter this place filled with warmth, hospitality and gaiety of a bygone era.

SMALL POINTS COTTAGE

The Small Point Cottage has a folklore history of hauntings dating back to 1971. Originally called Turner Cottage it was built in 1882 by Alanson and Ann Sheley and moved to its present location on Lake Shore Drive during the 1950's. It was the center for the Moral Re-Armament Development from 1956 to 1966. This is the only surviving Gothic Revival cottage on Mackinac Island. Gothic Revival was one of the first styles prevalent during the Victorian Era. At the foothills of Robinson's Folly, just east of Mission Point Resort, Small Point Cottage is about 3/4 of a mile from the center of town offering peace and tranquility from the daily bustling activity of downtown Mackinac Island. In 1971, John Findlay accepted a teaching position at the Mackinac Island Elementary School and moved his wife and seven children into Small Point Cottage, which was one of the largest and more insulated homes on the island at the time. Folktales indicate they experienced paranormal activity including items that would turn up missing, footsteps and unusual noises. Local folklore attributes the activity to be the ghost of a young girl who was forced to move away from the island, vowing that she would someday return.

However, one might imagine within the hectic Findlay household consisting of seven children, many items could have ordinarily been misplaces, footsteps in the night easily be attributed to children sneaking about after bedtime, and "unusual" noises and whispers merely normal household movement.

One of the first things to do when ghost hunting is to investigate the stories thoroughly to find out what else could be happening, as many times it is not ghostly phenomena, but normal every day occurrences. Ruling out the mundane in the beginning will save you time, energy and disappointment later on.

Upon my own investigation of Small Points Cottage, I found it lacking in any specific spirits. There did not appear to be any individual entity haunting this place. Whatever might had once haunted the Small Points Cottage, seemed to have moved on.

However what caught my attention was the energy surrounding the Small Points Cottage. It was very high vibrational, and seemed to emote Light and healing energy. I was entranced by the soothing nature of this place. It felt as if it was a place of healing for the weary traveler. I felt the soothing energy wash over me, almost immediately. Indeed there is something supernatural there, in the form of healing, providing a respite from the outside world. For those wanting to relax and drink in this extraordinary experience, The Small Point Cottage is the place to go.

Some places tend to retain certain energies, whether it is negative or positive. They appear to be a receptacle and will draw that particular energy to it. Places that act as negative receptacles seem to be much more prolific than locales that draw a high vibrational energy. The power of suggestion is great. If you think something is scary and negative, you fill that space with more negativity or fear. For many, hearing a frightening story about a particular place will increase that type of energy causing a percentage of people to swear they too experienced the phenomena, even if nothing is present. This is the case with the Small Points Cottage. When I channel from a sacred space of neutrality, I see the positive energy that has filled this piece of land, and building, and I hope those of you who visit it, will take the time to feel the magical vibrations that encompass this space, for Light energy is a wondrous experience that I would love for you to share!

It is important in ghost hunting to weed out such suggestibility within any reported paranormal activity, in order to get to the truth of the situation and to get the most accuracy out of the experience. A good example is if you try telling a group of people a graphic and detailed story about spiders. It will be easy to observe some of the listeners, begin to act as if something is crawling on them, even though there is nothing. Just as with your story about spiders, many times the suggestion of a ghostly presence will create fervor amongst the listeners that they are experiencing something that may or may not be there. There are many spirits on Mackinac Island it is up to you to decide which are real and which are mere tales to incite a reaction.

STONECLIFF ESTATE

In 1960 Mrs. Frances Lacey, a 49 yr. old wealthy widow from Detroit was found brutally murdered outside the gates of the Stonecliff Estate. Only the second murder to be recorded on Mackinac Island, the first being in 1910, Mrs. Lacey's murder was never solved. It has been reported that she had come to the Island with her daughter and son-in-law for the weekend, at their urging, as this was her first vacation trip after her husbands' death. Police reports indicate that she had made statements to her neighbor prior to her trip, that she had put her house in order, in case something were to happen to her. Police reports also indicated that Mrs. Lacey had left instructions with her daughter regarding the distribution of some personal items, "in case she died".[14]

She was staying at the Murray Hotel, in the center of the downtown area on Mackinac Island, while her daughter, son-in-law, and his sister stayed at his family's summer residence at British Landing, some four and a half miles on the other side of the Island. It was reported via the police report, that Mrs. Lacey was to have been walking to their cottage at British Landing that Saturday morning, taking the route along Lake Shore Rd, and after passing The Grand Hotel, (the scene of the 1910 murder) witnesses indicated they had seen her sitting on a bench near the fieldstone gate entrance of Stonecliff Estate (In 1960 this was the summer retreat for the Moral Re-Armament Society (MRA), a world-wide "fundamentalist" Christian organization.) resting perhaps, before proceeding to visit her daughter. At the time, a trail led nearly half a mile through the woods to the then sixty—year old English—style mansion. There, it turned out was to be her final destination. It is speculated that Mrs. Lacey was murdered at that spot as her body was found concealed in the underbrush nearby.[15]

After reading of the tales of the siting of a silent form of a woman standing and looking out to the lake, or sitting on the bench. I strolled to that area and immediately felt a strong sense of melancholy and sadness. It seems the earth near the murder scene has been scarred with this horror, and affected as it holds this energy, like a scar on one's skin. There seemed to be a pocket of cold air in a certain area. I was able to make a connection and sensed the feeling of someone standing by, simply waiting. Waiting for answers, waiting for others to know what happened. It was not a communicable spirit presence, as I felt Frances Lacey had gone on to a place of comfort and love. It was a loop memory phenomenon where a certain piece of the past continues to occur over and over again, without any ending. It is an imprint on the physical space where the tragedy occurred. The energy seems to take a picture of those feelings and it plays over and over for all who are able to feel it. This tape plays itself in image and sense of feelings, as at dusk I saw the outline of a female figure that simply vanished as I walked closer. Is this the same woman so dreadfully murdered on her holiday weekend? I leave that for you to decide during your own investigation. I leave that for you to decide during your own investigation.

THE GRAND HOTEL

What trip to Mackinac Island would be complete without heading up to the Grand Hotel? Built in 1887, the Grand Hotel was considered one of the finest examples of a summer resort of its time. Reports of unexplained phenomena at the Grand appear to be quite popular, yet I found no evidence or documentation of any current investigations or sightings. The stories remain as part of the history, but seemingly, without any witness accounts, documentation, or additional information. Heading up to the Grand Hotel on a sunny morning, I was looking to see for myself what truth lay in these stories.

In my research I found several comments indicating a belief that the hotel was constructed on land that was a Native American burial ground. In searching its history, no such reports of any discovery of human remains during construction have been documented.

Channeling in search of the type of energy that would indicate "sacred land disturbance" which is common in areas where Native graves have been moved or destroyed, proved futile. The only significant Native American energy I experienced was a sense of watching and waiting. From its vantage point high on the hill facing the lake, one can imagine watching the native canoes paddling home to safety. It is common to find this type of energy where people are looking out to the waters awaiting the return of loved ones.

Opposed to hiking up the long and winding hill in the summer heat, I climbed aboard a horse drawn taxi and found myself seated amongst a group of sneaker wearing, Bermuda shorts types heading up for the sumptuous Grand Hotel brunch.

I asked the woman with the beehive hairdo on my right if she ever heard of orbs at the hotel, as indicated in other books about the Grand. She asked if that was a type of dessert… Moving on to the man to my left, I inquired if he had ever heard of any ghost stories related to the Grand Hotel. He responded by asking if the buffet was "all you can eat"…. It seems not everyone is as aware of ghost hunting as much as I.

The feel of old time elegance combined with the bucolic beauty of the Grand Hotel, with its sculptured gardens, horse drawn carriages, and stately expansive porch was delightful to behold. Setting about my task, I located a lawn chair facing the hotel and settled myself in for a psychic 'look see'.

The first story, tells the tale of "the lady in black", who is said to have been a guest at the Grand Hotel. Wearing only black, with a veil over her face, the legend indicates she did not socialize and only left her room to walk her dog. To add to the mystery of this tale, it is said, she never spoke, and no one knew her identity. Stories include unsubstantiated tales of present-day guests have supposedly reported seeing her walking the grounds.

Paranormal manifestations of a repetitive nature, repeating the same activity unaware of the presence of others, such as walking back and forth on the hotel grounds, would indicate a place memory rather than an active cognizant entity. This type of manifestation is like a looping movie clip. It is more of an imprint or memory of an event than an active spirit haunting. Usually an energy "pocket" is present to indicate the presence of this type of place memory. In this case, none was experienced. There was also no entity energy of this woman in place at the hotel. I consider this tale nothing more than an urban legend, as there was no psychic evidence present to support this claim.

There are also stories of orb sightings in the main dining room. I was unable to locate any photographs to support such tales in books or websites. I took this claim to Robb Kaczor, a specialist in paranormal evidence, and he explained that 99 percent of all orbs photographed can be explained away, as either dust on the lens or in the air, or condensation, or reflections from light.

Considering all the various light sources in the main dining room of the Grand Hotel and the lack of actual physical evidence in the form of photographs or videos, this claim is easy to debunk. For an orb to be an authentic one, it has to be self-illuminating, as well as be seen with the naked eye. If it merely shows up in the photo, 99 percent of the time it is dust, water droplets or other natural occurrences. I am convinced if any of these authors had indeed photographed an authentic orb it would have been published in their books.

One of my favorite claims of a haunting at the Grand Hotel is that of footsteps, faint voices and doors slamming shut. These can be easily explained away as the cracking noises of an old building settling, the echo of sound due to lack of sound proofing between the rooms, and inner air currents present in long hallways, which can shut doors that have been left ajar. Without any investigative evidence, these are just stories used to increase curiosity and suggestibility.

In my research I came upon a story of a young girl, called "Rebecca" by some, who supposedly fell to her death from her hotel window, and who haunts the hallway on the fourth floor. Spirits connected to a specific place due to trauma have very distinctive energy. Upon investigation there were no signs of spirit activity or other supernatural manifestations or lingering energy found, from "Rebecca" nor was there any recorded evidence of her death ever found.

There is a difference between actual haunting and hysteria. Perception is reality to many people and what they desire to perceive may be the result of stories heard or desire to see a ghost. The Grand Hotel in my opinion is one of the most neutral places on the island.

It is by far a beautiful location, and a trip to Mackinac is not complete without a stay at this luxury hotel, and as said to me by my carriage mates on the way up the hill, "the brunch is to die for!" You will be pampered, by the very accommodating staff; the food is a gourmet delight and the scenery reminiscent of the Gatsby era. A definite must see for all visitors. But do not be afraid as there are no ghosts lurking by the doorways, or sneaking up behind you!

THE ISLAND HOUSE

The Island House is the oldest hotel on Mackinac Island in operation. Built in 1852, by Charles O'Malley, the hotel was a beach resort located along the shore. The second owner, Captain Henry VanAllen decides the hotel would have more room to expand if it was moved to its current location about 300 feet from the waterfront.

Until the late 1930's the VanAllen family owned and operated the Island House. When Rose VanAllen Webster, Henry's daughter, passed away the hotel was left unused for several years, then in 1945, the Moral Re-Armament organization used it briefly until The Island House's third owner, called, Island House Incorporated, operated the hotel. However, over the years, it deteriorated and was for a time at risk of being torn down. Harry and James Ryba, along with Victor Callewaert, purchased and restored The Island House in 1969. With them came a return to the old-world charm and sophistication of the original resort. In 1972, the renovations were completed, and it reopened.

Improvements continue at the Island House Hotel, including many modern amenities. The Island House is a great place to stay for those who enjoy classic styling with a modern touch.

Despite the lack of substantial ghost tales written about the Island House, I was strangely drawn there and decided on a weekends' stay. Upon entering the lobby, I enjoyed a lighthearted feeling of people filled with the expectation of fun vacations, talking excitedly about what to see first, their children laughing, and running about. Yet, it was early morning and the room was empty except for a lone clerk at the front desk.

After checking in, I meandered to the porch to sit and watch the sun dance over the waves, the boats in the marina rocking in slow rhythm, by the warm summer breeze. The band was playing a soothing waltz, and I casually commented to the couple sitting beside me, how lovely it was to have the hotel band playing during the day. The woman shot me a rather alarmed glance, pulled at her husbands' hand, muttered something about not knowing she was staying in a nut house and quickly left. I smiled to myself; this building was definitely alive with the past.

My curiosity peaked; I followed the sound of the phantom band to the dining room. It was set for lunch, yet empty of guests. I could hear the clatter of dinnerware, faint voices talking, and again the music from some earlier time. The feel was definitely the 1920's, and the energy was one of gaiety. Positive energy filled the room giving it a welcoming glow, compelling me to join the festivities. Pulling myself away from the ghostly revelry, I decided to run up to my room on the second floor to get my notebook. In my rush I almost bumped into the maid holding an armful of folded towels... I excused myself hurriedly and before bolting down the hall, realized something was strange about this maid. I turned but, she had already left. Returning to the hall after retrieving my notebook, the same maid, stood silently before me. Her uniform was mid-1920's styled garb and again, she smiled and nodded, as she walked past me, disappearing through the wall. Her presence made me want to learn her story and I decided to channel this spirit to discover why she was still here at the Island House.

During the channeling session, I discovered she was Rose's, personal maid, and continues to "tidy up" awaiting her boss's return. She indicated her job was to slip unnoticed through the halls, tidying up after guests, making beds and replenishing towels. Her instructions were to be as innocuous as possible, and remain unseen. I do not know who was more surprised by our encounter, her or me. Later that evening while looking at the old photographs that graced the lobby, I saw the same maid, standing next to Rose VanAllen Webster, in a group photo of the staff, wearing her uniform.

The Island House is a definite stop along your ghost hunting travels as it is extremely active with spirits, music, and a ghostly maid who will be sure to bring you extra towels.

Chapter 3

FAIRIES AND FOLKLORE

THE MYSTERIES OF MACKINAC ISLAND **are not limited to ghosts from the past. Getting lost along the trails and wooded pathways seems to be commonplace** occurrences for many visitors. Even the most experienced hiker can find themselves confused and disoriented at certain points along the trail, unable to navigate their way homeward.

From a psychic perspective the island possesses energy vortexes. There are also places where energy collide causing confusion and disorientation. Vortexes can be explained as potholes in the energy pathways. Ancient people knew that wherever the earth's energy gathered into a vortex was a sacred place. These strongly charged areas of the globe have also been the places where people have chosen to build churches, temples and other centers of spirit and learning. This could explain its feeling of sacredness to the Ojibwa people.

Mystics such as the Druids used song, sounds, and ceremonies to keep a chakra open, cleaned, and in proper working order. More and more people in the 21st century are remembering these old ways and are once again paying homage in ritual to the Great Mother. People are relearning the ancient shamanic and medicine way knowledge, centered on a relationship with the Earth. This not only helps heal the Earth, but affects the person strongly as well. The relationship between the Earth and us is reciprocal. We affect each other in direct and subtle ways. The Obijiwa intuitively knew this, and Mackinac Island is a place they worked their healing energy. As they meditated and prayed, they sent energy to the Earth and these vortexes served as portals to a higher dimension and increased the earths' positive energy flow. The Earth has energy layers. When we are close to an active chakra of the Earth, it energizes us to "see" things the way they really are—multidimensional and ever evolving. That is what occurs in areas of Mackinac Island. However because most people are unaware of this sudden change in energy, they can get confused and disoriented.

Native Ojibwe folklore explain it a different way in this popular tale.

"They were the bane of the giant fairies and the Indians that lived there, for the Indians believed they were behind every tree and every leaf, and were delighted to change the landscape to get them lost. The giant fairies avoided returning to their homes at night for more wine for their gatherings for fear that these tricksters would prevent them from returning to their gathering, by confusing them by changing the landscape.

Legend tells of small dwarf fairies that live in every tree, knoll, flower and rock on the island. The area tribes call them 'little dancing people' or 'Put-wuj-inn-ini,' who continue to be troublemakers to humans on Mackinac Island. The Put-wuj-inn-ini understands all that nature provides, but finds humans a mystery. It is said they find amusement in reactions of those who are lost, whether walking, biking or riding. They will move rocks, bushes, branches, or other natural landmarks to cause confusion. If you find yourself lost on the Island, remember that it's not very large and you can always find your way back to town. Your plight just might be the interesting afternoon entertainment for a supernatural creature."[1]

With much anticipation I head to the next place on my list, the Mission House. It is easy to see how fairy folklore has become so very popular as I look at the delicate flowers and plants along the pathway. It reminds me of the folklore told of the last gathering of the giant fairies that I discuss later in the book.

LAST GATHERING OF THE GIANT FAIRIES

Near the lake in front of the Mission House on Huron Street is where the legend of the Gathering of the Giant Fairies took place. According to local legend, it was originally used as a gathering place for the giant fairies. Tradition says that Mackinac Island, once the home of the Giant Fairies, enjoyed a rendezvous location at the meadow near the lake in front of the Mission House.

Pay special attention to the area across the road from the lake. If you relax and quiet your mind, you can feel the subtle energy change. It feels like a tingling of electricity. On a quiet summer night, the sound of a lone flute whispers softly on the evening breeze. The grassy area seems to remain indented, as if a reminder of the giant fairies who were once seated there. I found the area to the right filled with joyful and exuberant energy. Like seeing small children playing in the garden, one cannot help feeling like spinning with their arms spread wide. There is a heady feeling, one of being dizzy and lightheaded. It's unexplainable, but if you stand there for several minutes, you may feel it.

The folktale relates a story of an old Indian, who once camped near the home of the fairies. During the night, while he was asleep, a fairy spirit approached him, and beckoned him to follow. His spirit left his body and traveled with the fairy, and entered the mystical dwelling place of the spirits. Here, the Indian was introduced to the great spirits assembled in the solemn conclave. He was lost in wonder and admiration at what he saw around him.

The place where they were assembled appeared to be a very large and beautiful wigwam. After spending some time in the fairy abode, the master spirit of the assembly directed one of the lesser spirits to show the Indian out, and conduct him back to his body. What the proceedings of that assembly were, the Indian could not be induced to tell, nor were the particulars he saw during that mysterious visit ever made known to the native men.

Legend has it that Native Americans used the area in front of Mission Point as a burial ground as well as a summer residence. It was also used at various times, by the Moral Re-Armament movement, Mackinac College, and Mission Point Reserve.

Native Americans Folklore indicates Mackinac Island as the former home of a race of giants. The giant rock formation on the Island is said to be the only thing that remains of these giants. The story tells the tale of the last person presumably to see these giants, a teacher at the Mission House School, in the 1800's, his story, related below from Dirk Gringhuis book Were-Wolves and Woll-O-The-Wisps.

"One fine night, when the moon was full, Scholasticus, a mortal, sat upon the port of the Mission House drinking good wine. As his Indian companions retired for the evening to their wigwams and their fires put out, Scholasticus noticed what seemed to be giant fireflies swarming the flat near the lake. Then before him he saw the biggest man he had ever seen. This creature was 20 feet tall, yet graceful. He wore a cap of flowers and a dress made of tiger lily. A flower rose up, becoming a large tent and it was surrounded by many colorful fireflies acting as lights. The giant fairies came from all directions all of them very oddly dressed. Their garments were fantastical, bearing many exotic materials, what was assembling before him was a wedding. He watched them al with great wonder. Soon after much celebrating, they ran out of wine. Scholasticus felt sorry for them and tossed them a bottle of his own wine. In flight it grew as large as a hog's head. He startled the giants and one came to address him. He stated that he was a human brother and that they were the remnant of the first children of the earth and that their race was nearly extinct. He said this night was to be their last as living creatures and they would take shape and dwell in the rocks, boulders, cliffs and mountains. Never before had they let a mortal keep his eyes after witnessing a gathering, but that night they would allow it because it was their last gathering and he had been kind to prolong their cheer with his wine. So they welcomed Scholasticus and they all drank and the bride enjoyed a long dance with him. Suddenly a great splash of water came down around them, the giants cried out and fled, Scholasticus woke to kicking around on the ground with Martha the housekeeper standing over him with an empty water pail. He noticed that there were many wine bottles around him and thought he had drank too much. But for many evenings afterwards, waiting with plenty of wine, he sat on the porch awaiting the return of the giants. They never came for they had said they had met for the last time. But they may be seen in the rocks, guarding the home of the Great Spirit."[16]

There is definitely something unexplainable about the energy at that location. It almost flitters about as you stand there. Tiny little shreds of light glisten almost magically on the plants, and if you listen carefully you can hear the tinkering laughter of the fairies.

LEGEND OF ARCH ROCK

It is said that the Island of Mackinac is cavernous and its subterranean grottoes, halls and passages, known only to the Indians, were used as burial places for their dead.

This picturesque span known as Arch Rock is all that remains of the grand portal or entrance to the subterranean sleeping place of departed souls. Tradition tells us that this happened suddenly, a collapse of the earth, leaving the arch as it is. Never more shall the sacred dead be laid within the Great Turtle Island. It is said, the approaches to those revered and mysterious depths were forever destroyed and made impenetrable by a mighty bold of lightening.

Legend says that the moon's daughter Ad-dik-keemmaig loved Sis-kow-it, whos father was the Morning Sun. While awaiting the return of her brave warrior from war, she waited at arch rock, watching the direction in which he had left. They were to be married, and during her long wait she remained faithful, even though she was relentlessly pursued by a young Indian of a neighboring tribe. Her own mother, the Moon, conspired against her with the young Indian. She was to be captured and married before her brave warrior returned. When she realized this interlopers intention to capture her, she leapt from the arch, rather than be imprisoned by him. At the time of the warriors return he witnessed his bride to be in mid-flight. Looking down at her body, devastated, he asked his father, the Sun to witness the death of a brave man. He wrapped himself in her shawl and then leapt from the cliff.

Be careful when traversing the path leading to the rock as it has a strange energy that draws you in. There is something very spiritual about this place. A living monument to the dead, it takes on the energy around it changing the look of the rocks to reflect the mood of the day.

Skull Cave

Mackinac Island has some very colorful history in its folk lore. Legend has it that for countless years Mackinac Island, Michigan was viewed with awe by the Chippewa, Huron and the Ottawa as well as by their enemies, the Iroquois to the east, the Sioux to the west, as the first land to emerge from the waters at the time of creation.

Approaching the island in their canoes they were filled with superstitious wonder at the tall rocks each bearing a spirit of a mighty Man-i-tou. And it was here that the Great Spirit Git-chi Man-i-tou, who had formed the island, dwelt alone except for the giants in the rocks. Here he accepted the sacrifices and offerings. This sacred place was the burial area for chiefs and their families that they might be forever under his protection. Most believed the island was created for this very purpose. The legend tells of the white settlers who came and when seeing the harm they wrought upon his people Git-chi-Man-i-tou fled in anger and sorrow to the frozen north as the caribou had done before him, to live forever in the flickering flames of the Northern Lights.

Though the graves of the early Native Americans were never located those venturing off the main street will find cave like areas in the woods. The energy of the past warriors feels very strong to me at these places. It is said that there was once a web of tunnels throughout the island where the Ojibwa buried their dead.

The sense of burial rituals permeates my psychic consciousness; I can hear the soft beating of drums, and the wailing voices of women, especially at the area known as Skull Cave. I approached this sacred area feeling small among the massive rocks, the feeling to whisper is strong, as if I am entering a church. I arrive to see a band of children climbing over the "DO NOT CLIMB" sign as their parents eager for a photo opportunity, encouraged them onward. What a vast difference from its original purpose.

All this noise and gaiety seem in stark contrast to the gaping yawn of rocks forming the cave, forever frozen in time as a tomb for those warriors lost. Listen carefully as you stand before this memorial, can you hear the soft lilting tones of a magical flute? Though silent today, it stands forever with its mouth open, the recipient of more than its share of warrior remains laid to rest with honor and it is still a place of legend and mystery.

Skull Cave was once the location of a Native American burial ground, but the physical remains have long since been removed. The legend is of a musical pipe maker, Chief, Ke-nu, who was also a great leader, and warrior. His tribe depleted of unmarried men, due to heavy losses during the war, caused conflict within the woman of the tribe. Ke-nu decided to make these pipes to settle the fighting over who should marry the remaining warriors. It is said he took the red clay found on the Island with him to Skull Cave, the tribal burial ground, to make his pipes. As he worked, a skull from within the cave rolled to him and told him where to find copper tubes from which to make his pipes. With this material he constructed the musical instruments. After completing this task, he covered them in red clay. The skeletons in the cave began to play the pipes Ke-nu made. As they did so, they turned into living men again and followed Ke-nu back to his tribe and married the women, which stopped their bickering, and Ke-nu was happy once again. [16]

The legend says he took red clay with him to Skull Cave burial grounds where he could create his pipes in peace. At the entrance of the cave a skull rolled out toward him. The skull told him to dig up the ground at his feet and he would find copper tubes. With the copper he made his musical pipes. After completing this task, he covered them in red clay. The skeletons in the cave began to test the peace pipes Ke-nu made. As they did so, they turned into living men again. They followed Ke-nu back to his tribe, married the women, which stopped their bickering and Ke-nu was happy once again.[17]

Though no one can say with certainty, but this does appear to be the origination of the term "man cave".

Chapter 4

THE CEMETERIES AND GRAVEYARDS
ON MACKINAC ISLAND

MACKINAC ISLAND HAS ITS SHARE of burial grounds. First to be used as such was the Native Americans who considered the Island sacred and buried their warriors here in the hopes that they would find peace with Gitche Manitou, the Great Spirit. The locations of these graves have been lost through time, though in some areas of the island there is a definite sense of these souls, spirit guardians watching over the island.

Records do indicate burials of American and British soldiers, civilians, and Native Americans buried on the island in the early 1800's. Over time at least three cemeteries have been relocated and numerous Native graves have been found during these excavations.

Cemeteries and Graveyards have very definite energy all their own. For the novice it is probably the easiest location to sense spirit activity as there is so much in such a condensed area. Be mindful of its purpose which is to preserve the memory of those that once walked on this earth. Understand that not all the energy you may feel in these locations are positive, as not every person was positive and kindly. Remember one thing if nothing else.

Leave what spirits you find behind you and do not ask any to return home with you.

Mike G. decided to visit his local graveyard on Halloween and attempt a conjuring spell he read about. After conducting the ritual, he felt no spirit presence and went home disappointed. That evening to his chagrin his lights began to flicker, his kitchen cabinets began to open and shut repeatedly, as did his windows. He called me while cowering under his kitchen table with his pit bull, Bess. It seemed Mike's spell worked better than he expected. He had managed to unleash a very negative entity that attached itself to him and followed him home. Luckily I was able to clear the spirit out, with a sharp admonishment to Mike that he never tries that again! Judging by his pallor and abject horror over the incident I am confident he will heed my advice.

ST. ANNE'S CEMETERY

Saint Anne's Cemetery was first established in the late 1700's in downtown, off of Hoban St between Market and Main St., at the time it was right next to St. Anne's church (which was originally established at Fort Michilimackinac and brought over to the island during the revolutionary war.) In order to be buried here a person must be born on the Island or own property on it. The church was moved to its current location on Main Street in the 1820's mainly due to the cemetery becoming over crowded. Starting in the 1850's the new cemetery was cleared and it took over 30 years to move both the human remains and tombstones. In that time four graves were never moved to the new cemetery. The bodies believed to have remained at the Hoban Street location of the old St. Anne's cemetery, are Joseph Gleason, Abigail Legate, Elizabeth Mitchell and Mary Putoff.

Today, the Village Inn restaurant sits on the site where St Anne's Church was originally built and it is likely these remains are located under it or nearby.

Legend has it that a ghostly woman in a blue dress roams the cemetery and deceased family members of those whose graves were left behind have been seen walking the streets. At night in a macabre funeral procession seeking their lost loved ones. Upon entering the cemetery I am met with a sense of sadness and waiting. I was drawn to one particular corner where I sensed a very strong energy of longing. It did not appear to belong to any one spirit, just a general sense which is not uncommon in a cemetery where strong emotions are imprinted in the space.

POST CEMETERY

Post Cemetery has been in its current location since the mid 1820's, but due to poor record keeping the exact location of the first post cemetery is unknown. It is thought to be behind the fort, where other bodies have been found. Post Cemetery holds the remains of several Fort Mackinac soldiers and families. It is one of the three military cemeteries where the flag always flies at the half-staff.

In the rear left hand corner of this cemetery there are two children of Lieutenant Calvin Cowles that are buried. Isabel Hitchcock, Cowles d. 12 Dec 1888, and Josiah Hamilton Cowles, d. 4 Sep 1884

In 1884 Josiah died of a gastrointestinal disease at 5 months and 4 years later his sister Isabel died 5 weeks after her first birthday. Their deaths were especially hard on their mother Mary, who had lost a total of 3 children to disease. A woman in a long dress has been seen weeping over the children's grave.

The energy was very strong in this spot and I could feel the presence of a woman, and began a communication with her. She indicated her name was Mary, and she was French and her Husband Calvin was English. She blames her husband Calvin for the death of her children as she indicates she never wanted to come to the island in the first place. She found the weather severe and the living was harsh. A delicate woman of fine breeding, she struggled in this strange land. Her husband, a newly minted Lieutenant, thought this post would advance his career.

The death of her children was something she did not recover from and her spirit is still seen hovering over their graves. The area near the children's headstones felt much colder to me, than the rest of the area. There seemed to be a very soft muffling sound, not unlike the soft cries of children, or was it simply the wind? You decide.

Mackinac Island Cemetery

This cemetery, though not as written about in other paranormal books had a lot of spirit energy. Once located next to the Mission Church on Main Street it was moved in 1856 to its present location on Garrison Road, near St. Anne's Cemetery and Fort's Post Cemetery. This cemetery is still available for those who were either born on the Island or own property there.

As I walked through this small cemetery I was drawn to several headstones, husbands and wives, buried in small plots segregated from other families by lines made of small bricks. Their fences divided them in life and bricks separating neighbors in death.

I stood transfixed as a native women buried there at

my feet, began to speak. She indicated that many of the women of her tribe were married to soldiers. Not always of their own choosing. She shared with me that the women's' lives were difficult as they were expected to dress and act like the white women residing on the island, who did not associate with them. Therefore they were unable to learn the customs sufficiently and when they failed, as they often did, some were treated very harshly by their husbands. She did not like the clothing, the language or the way she was expected to act. She pointed out to me several other family plots, indicated her "sisters", and told me that they had a hard life as well. I asked why she remained in this human place, this graveyard instead of going to the Light. I was told that it was because of the Christian God of the husbands. It seems that these women were made to understand that in Heaven they would be with their spouses for eternity, and since that seemed more like a punishment, than a reward, they choose to stay together, here in this place on Mackinac Island, without their husbands, being free at last. She turned from me and as she did, I saw her join six other spirit women walking toward the woods.

This is a very worthwhile place to walk through on your visit to Mackinac Island, as the power of women is so strong here, as is there eternal presence of independence and strength.

Chapter 5

GHOSTS DEFINED

T HE STUDY OF PARANORMAL ACTIVITY continues to interest people worldwide. With the emergence of "ghost hunting" TV shows, the increase in the number of paranormal investigation groups and improvements in technology, more people are searching for the How To's of ghost hunting. "Where do I begin?" and "What do I need?" are the questions we hear. Before examining the How To's of a paranormal investigation, it is important to understand what you are looking for. Chapter 1 discusses the various types of ghosts; here we describe the different ways they manifest.

Most people are unable to see or hear spirits with their physical senses. Cameras and recording devices are able to document what our eyes and ears may not comprehend. Current theories indicate spirits are pure inter-dimensional energy beings, existing on a higher vibration, but with the ability to make contact with us. This is what you are seeking when ghost hunting; communication with something outside the realm of physical beings.

The goal in a paranormal investigation is to gain evidence in the form of photos, videos or voice recordings. However, not everything you get is going to be authentic evidence of ghostly presence. The first rule of ghost hunting is to leave your ego at home. Most of what you get on tape or recorded can be explained away as earthly activity. Ghost hunting for the most part is an activity where you sit around for hours in the dark waiting for an anomaly in the environment such as a sudden cold spot or heightened electromagnetic reading to appear on your instruments, so you can begin to take photos in the general area of the aberration hoping to get something viable. More than likely you will not see anything with your eyes. It is usually after the event when reviewing the tapes and recordings are you likely to see anything worthy of further investigation to determine if you in fact did get a ghostly figure on film, and not your teammate's shadow. Most times you will not get anything useful. But once you actually do get evidence of ghostly activity on film, it is exhilarating and exciting and you are hooked! Never again will you look at a shadow in the same way!

Spirits take many forms. This guide will help you understand the differences and enhance your ghost hunting experience. Of course everyone wants to experience a paranormal event during a ghost hunt, but be aware there is the risk of encountering negative or evil entities. I prefer to avoid being pushed down a flight of stairs, or slapped by an angry ghost. I do understand that feeling something paranormal can be exciting, but if you or your team members are experiencing physical harm, you may wish to consider getting out of there. Safety is of upmost importance. That being said, let's discuss the type of activity you may encounter.

Ghost manifestations can be divided into five categories: environmental anomalies, orbs, vortexes, EVP's, and full body manifestations. Knowing what they are, how to identify them and the most common explanations for each will get you started on your adventure!

Environmental anomalies are most commonly experienced. It is a way that a spirit makes its presence known and how the energy of its presence changes the energy of the environment. This can manifest as unexplained noises or seemingly random actions, such as footsteps, slamming of doors, lights and electronic appliances going on/off, or a sudden cold spot in a sealed room, or cold mist enveloping you. Cold spots are easily documented with technical equipment, and a good indicator it is time to turn on those video cameras and recorders!

Orbs are the easiest to capture on film, mainly because most of them are dust, pollen, rain, a bug on the lens, specs, dandelion seeds, spider webs etc.

A photograph of a true orb is a rarity. You didn't think this was going to be easy, did you? An authentic orb is a ball of energy. Normally white or bluish in color, one or more may appear on an otherwise normal photograph, and are occasionally captured on videotape as well (in which case they are usually moving, often at a high rate of speed.) A true orb can be seen with the naked eye, not just on camera.

The three rules of what constitutes an authentic orb are:

One: It appears as a ball, and is not a flat circle,

Two: It is self-illuminating

Three: It should leave a slight comet trail as it moves.

There is much speculation and controversy in the paranormal community regarding what composes an orb. Nonetheless a true orb is definitely a wondrous thing. Some say it is energy from the soul moving to the afterlife that has not learned to manifest in a more complex way. Others consider it a condensed form of energy with a low level intellect that appears as a random anomaly. Then there are those who insist it has a purpose, intellect and can be communicated with. There is even a school of thought that insists believes they are forms of extra-terrestrial beings. Strong evidence is lacking to support any one of these theories; no one has ever proven what an orb actually is, or if there are different types of orbs, or where they come from. I leave it up to you to decide.

When conducting a spirit release, I have seen orbs fly past. It appeared to me as the essence of the spirit leaving or moving about the space. Some prefer to think of it as a meaningless primitive form, but I have experienced them as having a purpose in their movements. Ones' opinion may depend on the orb and the psychic abilities of the person witnessing it. Many hypotheses and theories can be tossed out there, but we as humans can only guess, and through our experiences determine what they are.

When viewing orbs on film, be your own best critic. Try to assess if it is a natural occurrence like a flash reflection, airborne dust, moisture droplets or other glitch before claiming it is in fact an orb. Follow the three rules of what a true orb looks like. It can be disappointing to realize your orb is a technical glitch, or a natural occurrence, but it will certainly be less embarrassing than showing the orb photo proudly to others only to have them discount it as camera glitch. But keep taking those pictures and videos as you never know just when a real orb will fly into your photograph!

The next type of manifestation is an EVP or Electrical

Voice Phenomena. This is when a spirit voice is captured on a recording device. It can be as simplistic as a knock on the table, an animalistic sounding growl, or a human sounding voice speaking actual words. The EVP is seen by many as probably the best proof of spirit existence today. Paranormal investigators use this technique, and many have documented spirit activity through this method. You can try this at home, it is an easy process. There are two kinds of EVP's active and passive. A passive EVP is when the technician sets up the recorder, seals it in an empty room, and walks away, leaving the spirit to make contact through the device. An active EVP recording is an attempt at speaking directly with a spirit, although you will not hear an answer until you play back the recording, unless you are a psychic medium, and able to channel. EVP's are considered by many the best proof that something else was present in the room. The ear hears no response but when listening to the recording something is there. It can be as simple as a yes or no answer, and can progress to offering detailed answers or as ominous as a loud booming voice yelling "go away". This kind of recording is most indicative of an intelligent haunting, in essence a spirit that is actively trying to communicate. The device can be as inexpensive as a child's tape recorder, or as sophisticated as a professional digital recorder. Recorders with less fidelity, tend to produce more white noise in the background due to the low-quality microphone, as spirits are able to use the white noise to produce sound this can distort your evidence.

One of Robb's favorite EVP evidence was where several ghost tour guests were taped saying "I want to stay a while" and the very distinctive ghost voice in the background, said clearly "Just go". Another favorite was obtained at the Masonic Temple in Detroit, where the spirit was recorded growling loudly on tape, but unheard while walking through the room. It was so loud that it blocked out the EMF detector. (An EMF detector is a simple device used to measure fluctuation in the earths' electromagnetic field.)

Ectoplasm and Mists are the next type of manifestation. These are little clouds or wisps of light that can show up in photos. They may appear as a swirling spiral of light and sometimes take the shape of a seemingly opaque human form of considerable size. (See photo in Chapter 1) Spirits use energy to materialize. Orbs can be seen as a simplistic way in which they show themselves, and ectoplasm or mists, are seen as a more substantial demonstration. In the past ectoplasm was defined as a mist emitting from a psychic medium, usually from the mouth and covering a spirit in order to give it a physical appearance. At first being something more of legend and lore, the idea of ectoplasm was still popular, and eventually was used in plays, movies and books. Ectoplasm had a rise in cultural popularity after the movie Ghost Busters described green slime emitted by ghosts as "ectoplasmic residue." Most everyone who has ever seen the film can remember people getting "slimed" by the ghosts.

Today, ectoplasm in ghost investigations may be described as any unknown substance attributed to a haunting. Unlike orbs, ectoplasm, and mists are rarely seen with the naked eye, and most often are dismissed in photos or films as being a product of our bodies, a patch of fog, a reflection of light, exhaled breath, cigarette smoke or other natural events. Camera straps and human hair falling into the lens also help explain away most of what is caught on film. When a mist is present that cannot be attributed to moisture, fog, smoke, cigarette smoke, steam, or breathe in cold air, the vaporous cloud can usually be attributed to being a physical manifestation of spirit. Ectoplasm is also called ghost mists, ghost fog, or ghost vapors.

Unfortunately as with dust orbs, most photos of ectoplasm turns out to be a trick of the camera or something blocking the lens. For instance, when we breathe out we do not see the humidity we expel, when a camera catches it, it refracts the moisture, and shows up on film. A true picture of Ectoplasm is a cloud like fluidity but has solidness to it. It can also appears in the picture as a written message. Even the most experienced investigator, in a moment of excitement over his evidence needs to take the time to debunk his own photos before proclaiming them to the world.

The holy grail of spirit evidence is the Full Apparition. This is when the spirit appears as a fully manifested human figure. There are two ways this can occur. One is through manifest energy meaning the spirit is making it happen and it is witnessed in the physical, and the second theory is it appears as a psychic impression, seen by an individual's psychic eye. Both of these are valid.

Experiencing a full apparition of the first kind is a rare occurrence and on the wish list of every self-respecting ghost hunter. These images appear as a recognizable human or animal either fully or partially formed, or usually somewhat transparent. In some cases, the figure is clearly discernible to the witnesses, as a deceased friend or family member, making them even more valuable as evidence of paranormal activity. As discussed earlier, the most common experience referred to by witnesses is the awareness of a spiritual presence of a family member who that they discover later occurred at the very moment of that loved ones death.

Full body manifestations usually appear unexpectedly on photos, most commonly in the background of a portrait. For example, in a photo of a child, one may see her deceased grandmother's semi solid form standing in the background as if she is watching over her granddaughter. They can even appear quite solid and some seem to be interacting with the cameraman or while others appear oblivious to the camera. While it certainly seems that some ghosts are quite aware they are being photographed, there is no way of knowing whether this is true of all ghosts. When looking at photos that are said to be of full apparitions, it may be hard for the layman to discern whether these are authentic or not. It is exciting to think they are all authentic, but in reality most are not. If you are fortunate enough to have captured one in a photo, you indeed have a valuable prize!

As a psychic medium I am asked to investigate many unusual situations. In this instance the client contacted me about his encounter with a woman on horseback. At first he thought she was a neighbor riding along the trail between their farms. He was somewhat surprised when she did not return his greeting. As he continued to see her over the following month, he realized her clothing was not of current fashion, but mid-19th century and she always looked straight ahead, never acknowledging him. What he did not realize was that he was experiencing what every ghost hunter hopes to come upon: a full spirit apparition. His only concern was why it was there and how to make it go away.

There are many types of ghosts and various ways they

manifest. Now that you know what you will be looking for, it is time to put together your tool kit. Your ghost hunting equipment can be as extensive or simple as you like. In the next Chapter you will learn about equipment, some important rules to follow, and what you need to know to have some great adventures. Gather up your friends, equipment and remember some simple rules and you are ready to begin!

Chapter 6
GHOST HUNTING BASICS

I N THE COURSE OF CONDUCTING ghost tours to haunted locations Robb has frequently been asked, what is the best way to get started in ghost hunting? To answer those and other questions I sat down with Robb, to create this section. Robb has a wonderful way of cutting to the chase and simplifying what others seem to complicate. His knowledge is extremely valuable and provides the reader with a concrete step by step manual to use for their own ghost hunting adventures. After reading this section of the book you will be ready to take your own trip to Mackinac Island to see what you can find!

Just like everything you do in life, there is always a set of rules to abide by. Whether it is driving a car, riding a bike or what is expected of you in the work place. Ghost hunting is no different. Most of what you need to remember are the "CS's: or "common sense" rules, which surprisingly, people seem to forget once they are engaged in the thrill of the hunt!

Rule #1: Get Permission

Always have permission to be where you are going. Remember many places worthy of investigation are private property, and not all owners share your exuberance and interest in the paranormal. If you choose to ignore this rule, be sure to carry your ID with you, as the police will want to be able to identify the intruder, which in this case is YOU.

Rule #2: Buddy System

Go with a buddy or at the very least let someone know where you are going. Although the ghost may not hurt you, the environment you get into may be unsafe. Many of these locations are in old buildings and cemeteries, with trip hazards, possible live electrical wires, and floors not sturdy enough for your weight. To ensure your safety if you happen to have an accident, always carry your cell phone, and bring along the phone number of local police and hospital. Though the buddy system may not prevent an accident, in the least it offers you someone to summon help if needed.

Rule #3—Knowing when and how to leave

If something occurs to scare you, whether it be your own vivid imagination or an icy slap across the face or feeling that you are being consumed by a negative force; Get out. It is as simple as that. No need to be a hero. You are dealing with disembodied entities, and you need to understand that you may not always know what you have come upon or how to deal with it. It could be benign but it could also be something dark and evil. Do not question your flight instinct. Use it. That is what it is there for.

Rule # 4: Know your escape plan.

If you are scared, walk; do not run to the nearest exit, which you should have identified as part of your safety check upon arriving. To avoid injury and harm to yourself and others, as usually you will be ghost hunting in the dark, in unfamiliar surroundings, remain calm. Pushing and shoving does not make for a positive exit strategy, nor does screaming and scaring others or rushing the stairway. Always be aware of your surroundings and exists nearest you. Remember those ahead of you may not have seen or heard the thing that caused you to panic and therefore may be moving slower than you are. Also refer to rule #5 which will assist you if you have to execute rule #4. A ghost is unlikely to severely harm you. The most common assaults are pinching, slapping, hair pulling and occasion attempts at pushing someone down the stairs, all of which are survivable.

Rule #5: Ghost hunting is not a fashion show

Wear proper clothing and footwear for the environment you will be entering. Think safety first. Closed shoes, low heels are a must for most ghost hunting environments. Clothing should be close to the body, no capes or dresses, and of course no high heel shoes. Clothing items with pockets are helpful, as handbags simply get in the way. Many ghost hunters opt for hunting or fishing vests as they offer a variety of pockets to hold equipment. Cargo pants are also good. Remember ease of movement is important, especially in those cases where you are trying to exit quickly upon hearing or seeing something that frightens you. Comfort and practicality is the key. You never know if you will be crawling in an attic, or climbing around in a cemetery, and therefore you do not want to be hindered by your attire.

Rule #6: Know what you are getting into

No matter how much you have prepared yourself; experiencing a paranormal event can be disconcerting and frightening. But remember, you are participating in an investigation because you WANT to experience something otherworldly, otherwise you would not have chosen this as an activity to be involved with.

Rule #7 Respect for yourself and the spirits out there.

The point of ghost hunting is to gain evidence of spirit presence, make contact and document proof of existence. In all the excitement and thrill of the hunt it is important to remember that not every spirit or ghostly apparition is appearing or trying to communicate with you for your highest good. Just like there are negative and harmful people in this world, it is the same on the spirit plane. The biggest mistake I have seen even experienced ghost hunters make is to try to entice an entity to appear by taunting, bullying or insulting them. This never works to your benefit. Respect the spirits just like you would respect any other person.

As a medium I have been called upon to conduct spirit releases due to over eager investigators, and feel it is in your best interest to be aware of the possibilities of these occurrences, and how to avoid them, as being forewarned is forearmed.

During your adventures you may encounter a dark figure, either a shadow or full apparition; it is not uncommon for the figure to beckon you in some way to follow it. Or it may simply move slowly across a wall, down a hallway and stop and wait for you. Do not follow it. No good ever comes by following dark and menacing figures. In the spirit realm dark equates negative or evil, following such a thing is not going to take you to a happy place. I had a client who, when presented with this sort of entity noticed almost too late, it was leading him to the ledge of a three-story building!

Your focus on the entity, and its movements, combined

with the excitement surrounding the fact that you are making some sort of contact, means you are not paying attention to your surroundings. Always be aware of where you are.

I have seen spirit arms extending out of a wall beckoning for someone to take their arm and follow. I cannot repeat this enough, don't go with them. I liken it to walking down a dark inner city street. Would you follow a grimacing, evil looking man into a dark alley? Same common sense applies here.

Do not take chances with things you do not understand. Very few people have the tools and abilities to handle a situation such as this. Not all psychic mediums can manage it; therefore understand that you have a very slim chance to do so, yourself.

No matter what you believe, do not taunt or tease or try to anger spirits. Be very careful about using Ouija boards and other low level divination tools. It is arrogant and ignorant to assume that we know everything there is to know about negative entities, the afterlife, or any other area outside the earthly sphere, which is, after all, what "paranormal" means.

Evil spirits can follow you home and cause a myriad of problems, anywhere from knocking things off a shelf, causing discord between the inhabitants of your home, physically attacking you and others living there, as well as taking possession of your body. Yes, the need for exorcisms exists still today. I have been called upon many times to remove such spirits that have caused havoc due to the lack of common sense, respect and understanding that taunting something that has the intent to do you harm is far from a good idea.

Remember: You are there to observe and document ghosts, not channel or tease them. If you want to communicate with spirits, read my book on channeling, take my online class or bring a qualified medium with you on the ghost hunt. Otherwise be respectful. If you taunt a ghost to come for you, they just might. I always do a protection before I leave a paranormal investigation sight to ensure that nothing comes home with me. I suggest you do the same.

Rule #8: Be patient.

Usually nothing at all is going to happen for hours, if ever. Paranormal investigations mostly involve long stretches of doing nothing but sitting quietly and observing. Only embark on this kind of activity if you feel that the possibility of catching something extraordinary is worth a lot of time and effort. Study. Read. Watch. Learn. The more you know about paranormal history, other people's experiences, and the latest equipment and techniques, the more rewarding your experience will be. You do not have to subscribe to a particular theory to investigate the paranormal. Just accepting the premise that you do not know everything, and are willing to explore all possibilities and have a desire to learn, is more than enough to embark on this grand adventure!

Gathering up a team is your next step. There are many ghost hunting groups all over the world. It is easy to look online, email or make a phone call and join one. Working with more experienced investigators can offer you their experience as well as meeting a group of other people that enjoy this activity. Or you can gather together a bunch of your friends and set out to your nearest cemetery! Either way you will have fun!

Chapter 7

Gadgets and Gizmos: Your Tool Kit

OBB RECOMMENDS FOUR BASIC PIECES of equipment making it easy for beginners on a low budget to start out with as little expense as possible. These items are a voice recorder, still camera, a flashlight and your good old brain.

Any type of voice recorder will do. For the beginner, a tape recorder makes it easier to rewind and listen again. If you decide that ghost hunting is something you want to continue, spend the extra money on a digital recorder and an audio program for your computer, giving you the ability to download the recording to your computer and clean up the sound, making those disembodied voices clearer. Just be sure not to clean them up too far, because they start to sound like aliens instead of ghosts.

Purchase the best camera you can afford since it is an item you can use every day, not just in your nightly adventures in search of life after death. Do try to get a camera that has the flash as far away from the lens as possible. With the flash next to your lens those pesky fake orbs will appear in most of your photos. Trying to show people your flash produced orb pictures will identify you as a novice lacking in good ghost hunting skill. Remember

FRIDAY
JAN
13

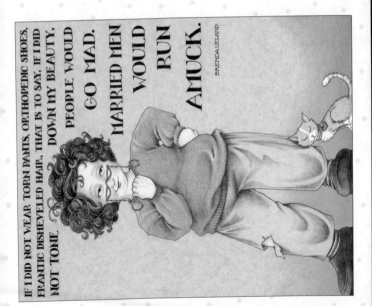

IF I DID NOT WEAR TORN PANTS, ORTHOPEDIC SHOES,
FRANTIC DISHEVELED HAIR, THAT IS TO SAY, IF I DID
NOT TONE DOWN MY BEAUTY,
PEOPLE WOULD
GO MAD.
MARRIED MEN
WOULD
RUN
AMUCK.

BRENDA UELAND

as we discussed most orbs are caused by dust, moisture or reflection. Very rarely will an orb photographed on film, be authentic. Also try and get a camera with the highest pixel count you can afford since the better the digital picture the less likely your eyes will start matrixing and picking out familiar objects where there is nothing to discern.

Your brain is by far the most useful tool in ghost hunting. Use it well and listen to that' voice in your head when it tells you to get out of a bad situation, as well as when to say "Ooooo, I have that ghostly feeling, take picture NOW!" Your intuition is your best guide, it will not fail you. Just listen to it!

Do not get discouraged when people come up with rational reasons why something you caught on film is merely a normal occurrence. That is how we learn. Every debunked photo helps teach you what to look for. Read every book you can on the subject of spooks, ghosts, and phantoms. Go for a walk in a cemetery, not because it's a city of the dead, but a peaceful place to walk and think about what you are doing and why you are seeking confirmation of the Other Side. Be prepared to look into your own soul and ask the hard questions, the ones that keep you up at night, "What if I'm wrong and all I am now is all I will ever be?" "Is my time on this earth the only time I have?" and "What if there is no life after death?" Those questions keep you honest and keep you on track to find your own truth, and your place in the universe! In any case I wish you well in your spiritual quest to seek out the unknown as it is a very rewarding challenge and fun hobby as well.—Robb Kaczor-

Ghost hunters use a variety of tools and techniques to investigate paranormal activity. While there is no universal acceptance among ghost hunters on specific methodologies, a number of these tools are commonly utilized by groups worldwide.

There are also a myriad of other you can purchase to add to your collection and we have listed and described many of them in the "Ghost Hunting Tools, Gadgets & Gizmos", list at the end of this book.

Chapter 8
CONDUCT YOUR OWN GHOST HUNT

THERE ARE VARIOUS WAYS TO conduct a paranormal investigation. Once a location has been determined, preferably one that has a history of spirit manifestation, and you have made arrangements with the owner if the location is on private property, it is a matter of hauling all the equipment and your team to the location.

It is always a good idea to get there before sundown to get a lay of the land before dark, as you will be unfamiliar with the terrain. A walk through in order to place the audio and visual equipment is your next step. Once you begin setting up, please keep safety in mind. For instance duct tape wires to the floor to avoid trip hazards. Locate all exits and make sure they are accessible. Divide the team up, spread out! There is usually much area to cover, and everyone can focus on a different place. Have the right attitude.

It is not necessary to believe in ghosts or spirits to conduct a paranormal investigation properly, but it is necessary to keep an open mind. A certain amount of skepticism is good, and will keep you from interpreting every little creak or speck of dust as paranormal phenomena. However, if you are convinced that nothing is going to happen, your mind will automatically discount anything that does occur, and you will not experience anything. Acknowledge that unexplained things do happen, but debunk whatever you can.

Performing a ghost hunt can take several hours, and in some cases several investigations, to find out the truth. Look for tricks and natural causes that explain seemingly paranormal phenomena as you perform your ghost hunt. Use fresh batteries and fresh film and have extra on hand in case you need them during your investigation.

Here is an easy to follow checklist:

1.Research the history of the property. Check deed records and search newspaper archives for mentions of the location or names of those who used to live there. This will help you clarify or make sense of any information you have obtained during the investigation. It's best to do this after your physical investigation to avoid the information corrupting any experiences you or your team may have during our time in the building.

2.Interview the individual who own the property or are having the paranormal experiences. Investigate if any other residents or family member can corroborate their stories. Get details such as the time of day, the sounds, sights and smells they experience. Ask if the witness is on any medication. It is not out of the realm of possibilities that the person is making it up, mentally ill, or due to certain medications is having hallucinations. Ask with tact and respect. They may indeed be having the paranormal experience but you will want to rule out all other possibilities. Just about every ghost hunting group I have spoken with gets several potential clients a year that indicate a spirit is sexually attacking them in their sleep.

Sexual attacks by incubus and succubus spirits are quite rare. The number of people seeking to share their so-called incubus/succubus experiences with ghost hunting groups, far outweighs the number of attacks. If the idea of this type of occurrence makes you uncomfortable, do not investigate it. This is a rare occurrence, and most times it will not be valid. Although many sexual attacks are reported to ghost hunting groups, after investigations it turns out these attacks are quite rare. If you do on the rare chance happen upon someone who is actually having this experience, you may not wish to put yourself in danger by having the spirit attach to you. It is best if you call a medium that is experienced with performing an exorcism.

Make a list and try to find other reasons why things occur, like banging water pipes or squeaky floors. This will give you a good idea of what to expect, as well as inform you and your investigative team which areas need the most focus and which areas your team should avoid. Remember that you and your team will be in an unfamiliar area in the dark, so if there are any dangerous or unique features in the home, you'll want to record them carefully.

3.Schedule a time in the late evening or overnight to perform the investigation. Though it is presumed that ghosts can be just as active during the day as at night, you're far more likely to record regular activity as opposed to paranormal activity if you conduct your investigation during the day.

4.Investigate the property in pairs. You want to make sure to put overly enthusiastic ghost hunters with more investigators to balance their personalities. Never let anyone investigate alone. This is not only for safety, but having a buddy also provides verification to any eyewitness accounts.

5. Set up battery operated recorders all over the area. Turn them on and let them record the entire time you're there to see if you can pick up any electronic voice phenomena, or EVPs, which are recorded voices that go unheard by the humans who are present at the time.

6.If you are investigating a large building, be sure to keep in touch with the other team members through walkie-talkies. Assign each team to a particular location, and then rotate after a specific time period so each member of the team experiences each location before the investigation closes for the night.

7.Sit quietly or ask questions to record Electronic Voice Phenomena (EVP). Many researchers believe that ghosts are able to communicate on wavelengths outside of human hearing, but digital recorders will pick it up and play it back within this range. EVP is one of the most fascinating and startling types of evidence and appears to be far more common than photographic evidence of the paranormal.

8.Tape down all wires and cords on the electronic equipment, and make sure every camera or recorder is securely mounted. Use a thermal imaging camera to determine heat fluctuations in the area that may not be discernible to you at the time. Keep it recording and pointed in front of you at all times. Try to find natural reasons for any changes you catch.

9.Set up cameras and voice recorders in the areas where most of the activity has been reported. You're not only most likely to catch evidence in these areas, but these are also the areas that the owners are probably most curious about and would like to have investigated.

Record everything that happens by stationing video recorders so they record as much of an area as possible, including the doorway. Make sure the view is wide enough to record the entire doorway to avoid skepticism if you do catch something. Also use hand-held recorders as you walk around the area hunting for ghosts. Sit quietly or ask questions to record Electronic Voice Phenomena (EVP). Many researchers believe that ghosts are able to communicate on wavelengths outside of human hearing, but digital recorders will pick it up and play it back within this range. EVP is one of the most fascinating and startling type of evidence and appears to be far more common than photographic evidence of the paranormal.

10.Take and document base readings of all the areas where you or another member of your team will be during the investigation. Record these on a notepad, include the location name, date, time and reading. It may also help to note who did the readings in case there are any questions later. Look for images or items that give you clues that people who live in the home practice black magic or witchcraft, as they're more prone to believe normal incidents are caused by ghosts, and more likely to have the ability to call in entities.

11. Duplicate any unusual readings on your equipment. It's always possible for a piece of equipment to malfunction, so you should always verify any event that seems to be authentically paranormal. Review all your information thoroughly and before reporting your findings to your client, get the whole team together to review the findings, check one another's' documentation and if you find something unusual, go back and try to recreate the situation to make sure it wasn't caused by others moving around during the investigation.

Paranormal investigation is a fascinating field, and can be rewarding on many levels. The key is attitude. Keep your mind open and be prepared for anything or nothing!

Conducting Interviews

Interviews are a very important part of documentation, as is keeping a file for each investigation, containing interviews, photos, audio tapes and any other evidence.

At least one person on your team should be responsible for interviewing witnesses to the paranormal activity at the location you are going to be investigating, particularly if it is a private residence. Interview forms are included at the end of this chapter.

Use one form per witness. It is also a good idea to record the interview on tape or digitally for future reference.

Confidentiality is important. Do not publish the name or photos of your witnesses without their expressed written permission.

Set up an interview time and location kthat is convenient for the witness. When possible, meet at the location where the experience took place. The witness will be able to show you exactly where the event occurred and other pertinent information at the venue. Take photographs of the relevant locations.

Never push a witness to talk about an experience they do not wish to share. Do not influence the witness's descriptions.

Allow the witness to remain anonymous, if they wish. NEVER give out a witness's name if they wish to keep it concealed.

ON YOUR WAY

You now have the tools, know the rules and we hope you are ready to go!

We have included a Ghost Hunting Tour of Mackinac Island complete with folklore to assist with your own paranormal investigations on the Island and offer you an opportunity to explore these places and discover for yourself

If you will see Harvey at Mission Point or hear the sobs of the lady in black? It is up to you to begin your own journey into the paranormal realm!

There is much we cannot explain in this world. Things that go bump in the night, bright lights that seem to take on a life of their own, shadowy figures, beckoning to be heard. We may never know where these come from or what their true purpose is. We can only learn to listen and try to hear them, for there is something here beyond our human experience.

We hope you have enjoyed this book and use it to help with your own discovery of the unknown and unexplained.

You probably picked up this book because you have an interest in the unknown and ghostly realm. We hope we have given you the tools to pursue your interest and discovery. And welcome you to the ghost hunting community. Only by having more people get involved can we truly understand the phenomena.

WITNESS INTERVIEW FORM

Date of Interview:
Interviewer Information:
Name:
Address:
Phone:
E-Mail:

Investigation Location:
Address of Location:

Name of Witness:
Wish to remain anonymous
Supplied name for research purposes
only—do not promote
Male / Female
Witness Info:
Address:
Phone Number:
E-mail:
Current Age:
Age at Time of Experience(s):
Date of Experience
Time of Day of Experience:
Exact place within the location of experience:

Was the experience: (Circle all that apply)
Visual Audible Olfactory Sensed Felt

VISUAL:

If the anomaly was visual, was it: (Circle all that apply)
Solid Transparent Vague Human
Male/Female White/Black/Color
Description of Apparition:
Clothing:
Facial Features:
Hair:
Height/Weight:
If not human, how large was it?
How long was it visible for?
Did the apparition: Disappear all at once/
gradually or simply move out of sight:
What action(s) did it make?
Did it attempt to make or make contact? If so, how:
Did the witness recognize the apparition?
Does the witness have an idea who the
apparition might have been?
If so, who?

AUDIBLE:

If an anomaly was an audible voice,
what did he/she/it say?
If the apparition communicated, did it
speak or convey telepathically?
Was it: (Circle all that apply)
Loud Faint Clear Muffled Male Female Androgynous

Curious Friendly Threatening Sad Responding/
Asking for a Response Close by Far away
Other description:

OLFACTORY:
Describe the odor:
How long did the witness experience the odor?
Other description:

SENSED:
Describe sensation:
Duration of the sensation?

FELT (PHYSICALLY):
Describe event:
Duration of the event?

FURTHER DESCRIPTION OF EXPERIENCE:

Download this form at:
www.joanstjohn.com/investigationform1.pdf

Investigation Form

Investigation Location:
Address of Location:
Date of Investigation:
Start Time:
End Time:
Investigators Present:
Weather Conditions:
Temperature:
Moon Phase:
Historically, this haunting involves: (Circle all that apply)
Visual Audible Olfactory Sensed Felt
Equipment Used:
Tape Recorders: (Type/Model)
Digital Recorders: (Type/Model)
Film Cameras: (Type/Model)
Video Cameras: (Type/Model)
Other Equipment (Type/Model)
Any experiences by team members during the investigation: (Have each witness fill out a witness form.

Download this form at:
www.joanstjohn.com/investigationform2.pdf

Chapter 9

Ghost Hunting Guide to Mackinac Island

Places to Go & Ghosties to See!

Bailey House—It has been reported that doors open and close and objects have fallen off of counters. Will you hear the sounds of boxes sliding across the attic floor? Or have you seen the figure of a woman peeking into the bedrooms of this inn?

Bogan Lane—A little girl with long hair is said to haunt this Bed & Breakfast. Perhaps you will hear her playing the Piano. It is said that guests have seen her, and heard her ask to go home.

Fort Mackinac—The guard house, jail, hospital, officers' hill and stone quarters are all promising locations to see paranormal activity. It is said that the children of the post commander supposedly haunt the officers' quarters. The hospitals near and in the fort are said to be haunted and are surrounded by what some call an "air of sickness, due to the many that died there. Rumor has it a skeleton was found in the "Black Hole" of the guardhouse and some people report a spine chilling feeling in the reconstructed guardhouse. Will you hear the phantom piper that walks on the stonework above the North Sally Port? He is only sighted on misty mornings and his music can be heard ever so faintly.

Grand Hotel—Stories of unearthed skeletons, ghostly figures, and spine tingling feelings have been reported at the Grand. One report indicated that not all the bodies in the old Post Cemetery were removed when the Grand Hotel was build, adding to the spirit activity.

Marquette Park—Any area of the island that had enough soil, was at one time used as a cemetery. When soldiers built a garden in what is now Marquette Park it is said they unearthed over 1000 sets of remains. Can you find any of the ghosts looking for their resting places?.

Mission House—When the Mission House, now state employee housing, was built it was at the heart of a Christian mission to convert the Native Indians who lived on the island. When Indian children became sick with Tuberculosis they were locked in the cool damp basement because it was thought this would help them. It didn't.... State employees report the ghosts of children who died there are seen in the basement and first two floors of the house. The attic is less haunted but people feel presences and items fall over seemingly on their own. The forms of children have be seen walking around often at night inside.

Mission Point—A story goes that supposedly, a high school student named "Harvey" had just been dumped by his girlfriend. He was so depressed that he jumped off the bluff behind Mission Point. He became a nuisance as people who worked in the carpenter shop would clean up sawdust, and it would be scattered around the place the next morning as if it has never been touched after work. Also, things would be moved to another place, or disappear. Other sightings included soldiers being seen walking around Mission Point's theatre and other places.

North Side—On the North Side of Island During the war of 1812, it is said that the English slaughtered 75 Indian men, since that time, people who live on Mackinac Island say that they see Indian men running through the woods at night, many tourists have reported several sightings of the ghosts of the slaughtered men.

The Rifle Range Trail—The sound of bullets fired over 100 years ago continues to be heard. It is said that a specter once appeared to a state employee who later identified him in an old fort photo.

Ruins of Stairway and Cave—On Mackinac Island there is a trail where below and slightly into the woods are the ruins of an old stone staircase leading up to nothing but two caves. While two explorers claim there got the chills just standing there, it was an eerie feeling. They took a picture of the staircase and they claim when the picture was developed a human sized black blur was in the center of the picture, atop the ruined staircase. The blur was interesting because of the way it was in relation to the lighting and trees and shadows it was obviously not a film defect, but rather something with "form" that was in the picture itself, but which they did not see while standing there. The shape was "in front" of some objects, but behind things in the foreground, suggesting that it was not a defect but something that was standing in front of and behind stones and trees. Today the stairs have decomposed quite a bit, and there is much crumbling down the side of the hill, but there is still a very definite "creepy" feeling suggesting that there is some type of energy present. It is one of the larger caves on the island. A great place to explore!

The Ghostly Rider—Some horse carriage drivers who make runs to and from Fort Mackinac after sunset have seen what looks like one of the hired historical re-creators, still in soldier costume, leaving work from the fort. He enters his carriage silently, and as it makes its way back to the stables, he disappears without a trace.

Ghost Hunting Tools
GADGETS & GIZMOS

Air Ion Counter—this device measures positive and negative ion in the air. Ghosts can cause a lot of positive ions because they give off high amounts of electromagnetic discharges. This is a great little add on!

Air Quality Monitoring Equipment—to assess the levels of gases such a carbon monoxide which are thought contribute to reports of paranormal activity.

Audio Recorders—Tape Recorder—or Digital and analog audio recorders are used capture anomalous audio, including voices and sounds that may be interpreted as electronic voice phenomena, which some theorize are attempts at communication by paranormal entities. A good tape recorder and an external static free microphone should be in use at all times during the ghost hunt. Even if you don't hear anything during the investigation, rewind the tape and play it back. Spirit voices have been known to be heard on tape later after review. This is referred to as, EVP, Electronic Voice Phenomena. Make sure you use brand new tapes when recording.

Bags—These should preferably be special plastic ones with zips, used to contain any material evidence that is found

Barometer—Some ghost hunters believe that paranormal activity can affect barometric pressure so it may be useful to take one.

Batteries—Extra Batteries—These are essential because ghosts are thought to be electromagnetic and this can cause batteries to run down quite quickly. Extra batteries will be essential for all of the ghost hunting equipment that needs it.

Candles & Matches—These are essential items especially if your flashlight and equipment stop working. Some ghost hunters believer that ghost energy can drain equipment energy and candles should be taken as a backup. Sometimes candles may be used but don't count on them staying lit, as ghosts like to blow them out.

Cell Phone—These are useful in case of an emergency they can also be affected by the presence of strange activity

Compass—A great tool for navigation if you know how to use one and also great for picking up those electromagnetic forces. A compass will react to any magnetic or electrical stimulus that is out of the ordinary. Same rules apply here, try not to use the electronic compass's. Stick to the simple boy scout, "needle points North" version.

Control Object—This is a small object such as a coin that is placed on a piece of white paper, which in turn is placed on a table or where it will not be disturbed. A pencil circle is drawn around the coin so that it's exact location is recorded. The coin and paper are then left and then re-examined at the end of the ghost hunt to see if the coin has moved. If it has, then this could indicate some strange activity. Ensure no-one can accidentally move the coin or you will obtain false results.

Digital Recorder—These are very useful and they are quickly becoming the item of choice for obtaining electronic voice phenomenon results.

Dowsing Rods—Some researchers feel that the use of dowsing rods can help to pick up ghosts.

EMF Detectors (K2 Meters)—is a simple device used to measure fluctuation in the earths' electromagnetic field. As a spirit draws energy to manifest, it creates fluctuations that set off the EMF detectors. Also High EMF areas include power lines, faulty wiring, electric devices such as air purifiers refrigerators, TVs, which, can affect the health and wellbeing of the people subjected to them. We use EMF detectors far more often to debunk the presence of a spirit rather than to prove the existence of one. EMF Detectors can pick up electronic fields over different frequencies. Where there are ghosts there are usually disruptions in the electronic field. These are a must for field work. As a guideline each person in your group should have their own. This is an inexpensive, widely available and helpful tool for a budding ghost hunter.

Film—Some investigators prefer using cameras with film rather than digital. If you use film be aware that electromagnetic discharges can affect film and it may need to be replaced. Therefore it is important to ensure that plenty of spare rolls are accessible. Use 200 or 400 possibly 800 speed film, this will provide the best photographs.

First Aid Kit—We hope you will never need it, but it is a practical and pragmatic thing to have along.

Flashlight—Ghost hunting is mostly done at night. A flashlight is necessary for your own safety. Batteries are not always reliable in areas where there is spirit activity as spirits have a tendency to drain batteries. Bring extra batteries, or purchase a flashlight that has a crank to wind to charge the battery. Always have bright flash lights (usually 3 or 4) and extra batteries.

Geiger counter—to measure fluctuations in radiation which some believe will point to a disturbance in spirit energy

Ghost Catcher—also called, a Spirit Wind Chime) The idea here is that the spirit will pass by and cause the ghost catcher to chime much like a wind chime does in the wind. A store purchased one can be used if they are very lightweight.

For obvious reasons these will not be affective outside or in any area where a breeze or wind is blowing. You can make Ghost Catchers yourself. Take about 8 to 10 very thin strips of metal (about one inch wide and about 6 to 8 inches long). Put a hole in one end of each strip. Tie separate strings to each strip. Leave about 6 inches of slack in the string and tie the other end of the strings to a pole or something that keeps the strips hanging down. Tie them about one half inch apart on the pole. The strips shouldn't touch each other but shouldn't be very far apart either. Hang the pole from the ceiling or in a doorway. I know that some people paint the strips with glowing paint to make them easier to see at night or in the dark. Any variation on a wind chime will work. For the best results make several ghost catchers and put them at different spots throughout a house.

Headset Communicators—When you have a team of three or more people headset communicators are a great idea for staying in contact when spread out over a distance. You can use the hand held walkie-talkies types but the headset frees up your hands for holding cameras etc.

Hydrometer—his device is useful for picking up any changes in air humidity.

Infrared and/or Ultrasonic Motion Sensors—are used to detect possible anomalous movement within a given area, or to assist in creating a controlled environment where any human movement is detected.

Infrared or Thermal Camera—Infrared and thermal cameras, imaging video cameras, and/or hand-held infrared surface and ambient temperature sensors detect changes in the environment, such as "cold spots", which some believe accompanies paranormal activity. Still and video photography using infrared, digital, night vision, and even disposable film cameras can capture evidence of possible visual manifestations, such as orbs, mist, apparitions, and ectoplasm.

Infrared Thermal Scanner—This item saves on infrared film and your time by accurately pinpointing the cold spots. These scanners are excellent to use in outside investigations. This is not something that you must have, but if you can afford, it give it a try. This is excellent for use in outside investigations.

Microphone—A good microphone is essential for picking up electronic voice phenomena.

Motion Detectors—These devices are good for sensing movement when there should be none. One sensor can easily monitor an entire hallway or room. it is an ideal tool for indoor investigations

Negative Ion Detectors—This will detect an excess of negative ions which some feel are associated with paranormal activity

Night Vision Equipment—Night Vision scopes can be very useful. You can also get reasonably priced adapters that will attach the scopes to video cameras.

Night Vision Video Camera—This device is similar to combining a video camera with a night vision scope and allows the recording of light not normally visible to the naked eye. A good investigative tool

Notebook—Always keep records of times and events, this is very useful for documenting the investigation and especially if the study is to be replicated. Pens and pencils are also essential.

Red Cellophane—This is a useful material for covering the lenses of flashlights in order to prevent the light from being too blinding.

Small Wind Chimes—Some researchers claim that breezes sometimes accompany ghosts. Wind chimes should be placed in areas where the ghost is thought most likely to appear and of course out of the wind or drafts. This is a simple system that can alert investigators to photograph the area.

Spotlights—Small battery powered spot lights really help at night when it comes to setting up and taking down cameras and other equipment. They can also be used for safety and to get a better view of the surrounding terrain at night. Get the lights that sit on the ground but have swivels on the lights to set them to different angles. You will do well to purchase between two and six spotlights depending on your needs.

Still Camera—The best kind of camera is a 35 millimeter digital camera. A higher picture quality is obtained without artifacts that can lead to false ghost images such as: mist being thought to be orbs, or streaks of light on the film mistaken for ectoplasm or the ever popular "vortex" otherwise known as the unnoticed untethered camera strap, most of which can be explained away. A 35mm camera with black and white film and/or infrared film is very useful for capturing any pictures. Ensure that you have plenty of film. For best results use a film speed of no less than 200. A speed of 800 may produce better results although it will be very grainy. It is also important that your camera has flash either its own or slave flash. Video or camcorders are also very good and should be used. Use brand new tapes. Don't use an old tape and tape over something. Have all the film developed by experts and don't forget a tri-pod to avoid camera shake.

Talcum Powder—This is a useful substance for capturing footprints or handprints. Sprinkle it around on the ground around where the investigation is taking place.

Tape Recorder—A good tape recorder preferably digital, and an external static-free microphone should be in use at all times during a ghost hunt. It records what you may not be able to hear with your ear, and is a valuable tool if you are interested in documenting EVP activity.

Thermal Imaging Scopes—This device allows you to actually see what your thermal scanner detects. Should there be a cold spot, this infrared technology makes it possible to see the shape and size of the cold pot. Unfortunately this is still quite expensive equipment. Buy at the Ghost Hunter store.

Thermometer—A good room thermometer can detect changes in room temperature. Rapid drop in temperature has often been associated with the presence of a ghost It's best to use the old fashion mercury filled, red line, thermometers. They have electronic thermometers but in ghost cases where electromagnetic forces have been reported they might fail right when you need them.

Video Camera—This piece of equipment allows events to be captured as they are happening.

Voice Recorder—Any type of voice recorder will do. Tape recorders are generally easier for rewind purposes, but digital can be uploaded easier to the computer.

Walkie-Talkies—These devices allow you to communicate with your ghost hunting party. If you are investigating a house and you have people scattered all over, walkie-talkies allow you to keep in touch

Watch—An essential piece of equipment for recording the time when the events happen.

Glossary of Terms

Afterlife—(also referred to as life after death or the hereafter) is the idea that the consciousness or mind of a being continues after physical death occurs. In many popular views, this continued existence often takes place in an immaterial or spiritual realm. Major views on the afterlife derive from religion, esotericism and metaphysics.

Agent—A person who attempts to communicate information to another person in an ESP experiment, or is the subject in a psychokinesis experiment. Also refers to the person who is the focus of a poltergeist activity.

Amorphous—Having no definite form or shape, spirits and ghosts often appears in mist-like forms or shapes.

Anomalies—Deviation from the norm

Apparition—A phenomenon where a spirit, takes on a physical form that can be seen and photographed. It can take the shape of a human, animal or undistinguishable shape.

Apport—The arrival of an object during a séance or a haunting. These can be animate or inanimate.

Asport—The disappearance of objects that reappear elsewhere or not at all.

Astral Body—A term to refer to a supposed "double" of the person's physical body. The astral body is believed to be separable from the physical body during astral projection (out of body experience) and at death.

Astral Plane—A plane of existence where souls reside on their way to being born and after death,. It is generally believed to be populated by angels, spirits or other immaterial beings.

Astral Projection—When the spirit travels outside of the body either to the astral plane or another location on this plane. Also known as Out of Body Experience or OBE.

Aura—Is an emanation of energy which surrounds all living things. Many with psychic abilities are able to see and interpret this energy.

Automatic Writing or Automatic Art—Is the ability to freely channel your higher self or another souls' words, music, or art without the interruptive interference conscious thought. It is believed to be a way of communicating with those on the other side.

Automatism—A process in which the subconscious communicates with the conscious by means of a vehicle such as a Ouija Board, automatic writing or pendulum swinging.

Benign Spirit—A spirit that is not harmful

Channeling—The process by which a medium communicates information from non-physical beings, such as spirits, deities, demons or aliens through entering an altered state of consciousness to obtain information. There are two types of channeling; conscious channeling where a medium speaks with a spirit and conveys the information to others, or a trance channel where the spirit inhabits the body of the medium and talks directly through the medium. The mediums' is actually out of body at the time, and their body takes on the attributes and mannerisms of the spirit. This is something that should only be done by qualified and experienced mediums only.

Clairaudience—Hearing voices, astral music or discarnate beings, inaudible to the normal human ear.

Clairsentience—The obtaining of information using faculties other than vision or hearing. It is the ability to clearly feel yours and/or another's emotions and sensations.

Clairvoyance—Clairvoyance is the psychic ability or power to see objects, and visions, or to gain information beyond the range of natural vision, or vision assisted by technology. This is a form of extra-sensory perception, and information from past, present and future may be garnered from those with this ability. To have lucid mental perceptions and keen insights about people and life situations and to have clear visual mental images, pictures, to "see" auras and other psychic phenomena.

Cleansing Prayer—A practice to cleanse the spiritual vibrations which drive the inferior or lower level energy forms form a person or area. This is used as a protection ritual before a medium communicates with disincarnate beings.

Cold Spot—Describes an area of localized coldness or a sudden decrease in ambient temperature that is allegedly connected to paranormal activity. Some ghost hunters warn against using cold spots as a paranormal indicator alone, because cold spots can often be explained by natural temperature variances.

Collective Apparition—An ghostly apparition seen by several people at the same time.

Deep Trance Medium—Otherwise known as trance medium or trance channeler. A psychic medium who allows a spirit entity to enter their body and communicate using the mediums vocal cords.

Demonic Spirits—An entity or spirit spawning

from the devil that is or was of this earth. They have the capability of human possession, and the strength greater than any flesh and blood creature. Usually demonic spirits are distinguished by their dark, or black masses of psychic energy.

Direct Voice—A voice heard in a seance which does not seem to emanate from any person. The voice may seem to come out of thin air, or from a trumpet used specifically for this purpose.

Discarnate—A spirit that exists without a physical body.

Disembodied—A spirit that is functioning without a body

Disembodied Voice—A voice that is heard, without coming from a physical being, also known as EVP.

Divination—The various methods of obtaining unknown knowledge or future events using such things as a pendulum, tarot cards, runes, Ouija board, divining rod or other outside forces.

Divining Rod—A tool used in the act of dowsing, most famously known as a—shaped tree branch, but may be "L" shaped, may be wire, metal, brass or even glass or plastic. Dowsing is the practice of searching for water, minerals, gemstones or other naturally occurring objects underground by holding and interpreting the movement of the rods. It is also very useful in detecting spirit activity.

Ectoplasm—A viscous white paranormal substance which is said to be emitted by physical mediums when in a trance state. This material is excreted as gauz-like substance from orifices on the medium's body and spiritual entities are said to drape this substance over their nonphysical body, enabling them to interact in our physical universe. It is considered a product of psychic energy which usually forms as a fog like mist, solid white mass, or vortexes.

Electromagnetic Field (EMF) An electric and magnetic energy that radiates from radio and light waves to gamma and cosmic rays.

Electromagnetic Field Meter (EMF)—A tool that detects the changes in the Electromagnetic Field. The normal reading for paranormal activity is between 2.0 and 8.0. Above this is usually man-made in origin.

Empath—Someone who shows considerable empathic ability psychically.

Entity—The force or principle of life that animates the body of living things; an incorporeal being, the soul of a dead person.

ESP—Extrasensory Perception—The ability to perceive things without the aid of the five senses, i.e. with the mind alone or with supernatural assistance. It is communication or perception by means other than the physical sense perception or communication outside of normal sensory capability, as in telepathy and clairvoyance. It is also known as second sight, or sixth sense.

Evocation—The summoning of spirits by usage of ritual, gesture or verse of incantation.

EVP—stands for Electronic Voice Phenomena. The use of audio equipment to capture voices and sounds of the dead where there are no physical presences in the area where the recordings are being taken. These voices are not heard by the normal human ear but upon listening to the recordings. A phenomenon discovered by Konstantin Raudiv. If a spirit voice is heard at any other time audibly, recording or not recording, this would be called an 'audible disembodied voice.

Exorcism—The act of expelling unwanted ghosts,

spirits, demons, or other entities believed to be disturbing or possessing a person or a place that people frequent. Not something to be done by the uninitiated or novice.

Extra-Terrestrials—Life forms originating on planets other than our own.

Gauss Meter—A device that is used to measure the electromagnetic field, also referred to as EMF detectors or magnetometers.

Ghost—A ghost is believed to be the soul or life force of a person.

Haunted—A person, place or an object to which a spirit is attached. The spirits can be human or inhuman in nature.

Haunting—Paranormal phenomena such as apparitions, unexplained sounds, smells or other sensations associated with a particular object, or location. Most commonly a spirit or ghost that tries to make itself known for a variety of reasons, that can include, asking for help, protecting a loved one, or feeling they have unfinished business.

Holy Water—Water that has been blessed by a member of the clergy. Holy water is said to have the ability to negate negative forces.

Incubus—A demonic entity capable of sexually arousing and sometimes assaulting women.

Indirect Voice—Mediumistic phenomenon in which the discarnate entity appears to speak using the vocal apparatus of the medium. Often the voice will sound very different from the medium's normal voice.

Kirlian Photography—The photographing of the human aura. Two Russian scientists, Semyon and Valentina Kirlian founded this process.

Levitation—The raising of a person or object into the air without any visible means.

Malevolent Spirit—A spirit that wishes to do harm.

Malicious Spirit—These spirits will destroy or damage things of a personal or financial value for the sake of hurting others.

Manifestation—The appearance or taking of form, of an entity.

Materialization—The formation of a visible physical form of a spirit.

Matrixing—When the mind attempts to manifest images as something they are not.

Medium—A person who is said to have the ability to communicate with the dead.

Metaphysics—The study of that which is beyond the laws of physics.

Near-Death Experience (NDE)—Experiences of people afer they have been pronounced clinically dead, or been very close to death.

Necromancy—The practice of communicating with the dead to obtain knowledge of the future, others' secrets, and so forth.

Occultism—Esoteric systems of belief and practice that assume the existence of mysterious forces and entities.

Orbs—A spherical shaped, translucent mass of energy resembling a ball or globe of light.

Ouija Board—A game board that is used to communicate with low level spirits.

Outward Manifestation—The physical manifestation of paranormal activity.

Paranormal—That which cannot be explained away by

science. Commonly used term to refer to such occurrences as spirit sightings and activity denoted as "haunted: i.e.: in houses and other buildings. The term Paranormal may also be used to refer to any psychic/telepathic activity. Events or abilities outside the range of normal experience that remains unexplained by established science.

Parapsychology—Refers to the scientific study of paranormal phenomena.

Phantom—An apparition or specter. Existing only as an energy form.

Phantomania—Paralysis that occurs when someone is under attack from supernatural or prenatural forces, also known as psychic paralysis.

Planchette—The triangular instrument used as a pointer to answer questions on a Ouija board.

Poltergeist—A general term applied to a variety of physical phenomena. These can include temperature variations, anomalous sounds, and movement of physical objects. The word 'poltergeist' literally means 'noisy spirit' in German, and was coined back when such phenomena were thought to be due to the presence of some sort of mischievous entity. Currently, poltergeist phenomena are usually considered to be related either to unusual physical conditions at the affected site, or to be related to psychokinesis. Anecdotal reports suggest that many poltergeist focuses on an individual under some form of emotional stress.

Possession—An altered state of consciousness in which the conscious personality of the individual is replaced with that of another personality thought of as a possessing entity. The cure is an exorcism.

Precognition—Knowledge of pending future events.

Premonition—Feeling or warning about a future event. This may be a vague feeling or it can be quite specific.

Psi ball—a ball of energy made by using Elemental energy.

Psychic—A person with Popular term used to denote a person who regularly uses, or who appears to be especially gifted with, the ability to see, hear and feel by use of senses other than the natural senses

Psychic Attack—An attack that can either be physical or mental by a spirit or psychic energy.

Psychokinesis—is the paranormal influence of the mind on physical events and processes. The movement of matter, also referred to as telekinesis, refers to the direct influence of mind on a physical system that cannot be entirely accounted for by the mediation of any known physical energy (i.e. moving objects with the mind.

Psychometry—The art of sensing the history, creator or owner of an object by touch and psychic perception.

Pyrokenesis—setting something on fire using energy produced by ones mental powers.

Reincarnation—The belief that some aspect of a persons' being survives death and can be reborn in a new body at some future date.

Remote Viewing (RV)—Seeing or perceiving objects or locations at a distance, using only the mind, or through an out-of-body experience. Ability to access distant or shielded information primarily of visual character, such as natural or structural features, via an unknown mental process. RV can include other sensory modes, such as feelings, motion, or sound. Some individuals associate specific approaches, or protocols, with RV. Other similar terms: remote perception, enhanced perception, extrasensory perception (ESP).

Residual Haunting—believed to be a psychic imprint of a scene that keeps repeating itself. With this type of haunting no active interaction with the ghost occurs.

Retro cognition—Paranormal knowledge of past events.

Retroactive Psychokinesis—Paranormal influance that an agent can have on an experiment after it has been completed.

Scrying—A form of divination performed by gazing into a reflective, translucent or luminescent surfaces such as a crystal ball, black mirror, smoke, fire or water.

Séance—A meeting, often led by a psychic/medium, at which people attempt to make contact with spirits who have passed onto the other side.

Shape-Shifting—The paranormal ability to assume the form of another person, an animal or other entity.

Sleep Paralysis—A state of seeming to be awake but unable to move.

Specter—A ghost or apparition that exists only in appearance as with a phantom.

Spirit—Is often used to refer to the personality of a deceased individual. The spiritual element or divine essence of a person, generally believed to be immortal. It is believed that spirits exist in a higher vibrational space and can only be seen under certain cirucmstances or by people with special abilities.

Subliminal Perception—Perceiving without conscious awareness.

Succubus—A demonic entity said to inspire lust in men and then assaulting them.

Supernatural or paranormal—Beyond the normal. Inexplicable in terms of our ordinary understanding or current scientific knowledge.

Telekinesis—The movement of objects by scientifically inexplicable means believed to be achieved solely through the mind.

Telepathy—Communication of one's mind with another by means other than the normal senses.

Teleportation—Paranormal transportation of objects to a distant place.

Thermal-Imaging Digital Camera—A Thermal Imaging Camera is a type of thermo graphic camera. By rendering infrared radiation as visible light, such cameras allow the user to see areas of heat through darkness. Thermal imaging cameras are typically handheld, but may be helmet-mounted. Thermal imaging cameras pick up body heat, and they are normally used in cases where people are trapped where rescuers cannot find them.

Vortex—A mass of fluid or air in a rotational movement, such as a whirlpool. Often used to mean a mysterious disturbance or opening to another realm. They can also appear long and narrow and having a tread like design. Some theorize this is a vehicle to transport spirits the the shape of orbs from their realm to ours.

White Noise—White noise is a random signal (or process) with a flat power spectral density. In other words, the signal contains equal power within a fixed bandwidth at any center frequency. White noise draws its name from white light in which the power spectral density of the light is distributed over the visible band in such a way that the eye's three color receptors (cones) are approximately equally stimulated. Strong white noise also has the quality of being independent and identically distributed, which implies no autocorrelation. In particular, if rt is normally distributed with mean zero and standard deviation σ, the series is called a Gaussian white noise. Basically this is a hiss-like sound formed by combining all audible frequencies.

1. Keister, Doublas-Stories in Stone: A Field Guide to Cemetery Symbolism and Iconography, Gibbs Smith Publishing (2004)

2. Gringhuis, Dirk- Lore of the Great Turtle, Mackinac Island State Park Commission, Mackinac Island, MI

3. Jacques Brunius, "Ectoplasm," in Encyclopedias Da Costa [1947], available as part of Encyclopaedia Acephalica (London: Atlas Press, 1995).

4. Oliver Lodge, Ether and Reality (London: Hodder & Stoughton, 1925).

5. NeuroQuantology- An Interdisciplinary Journal of Neuroscience and Quantum Physics. Vol.6, No. 2,(2008) Synaptic Quantum Tunnelling Entropy Increase in Vacuum: A Conjecture About the Mechanism of Poltergeist Phenomena

6. New Scientist Physics & Math HYPERLINK "http://www.newscientist.com" www.newscientist.com 01.04.2008

7. Poltergeist (1972), Theory and Experiment in Psychical Research (1975), Psychic Connections (1995, with co-author Lois Duncan), and Unleashed: Of Poltergeists

and Murder: The Curious Story of Tina Resch (2004, with co-author Valerie Storey).

8. NeuroQuantology- An Interdisciplinary Journal of Neuroscience and Quantum Physics. Vol.6, No. 2,(2008) Synaptic Quantum Tunnelling Entropy Increase in Vacuum: A Conjecture About the Mechanism of Poltergeist Phenomena

9. Encyclopedia of Psychic Science. London: Arthors Press, 1934 Nandor Fodor

10. Gauld, Alan-Poltergeists, with Tony Cornell (1979)

11. Investigating the Paranormal By Tony Cornell

12. Roll, W. G. (1968). Some physical and psychological aspects of a series of poltergeist phenomena. Journal of the American Society for Psychical Research, 62, 263-308.

13. The Haunted Mind: A psychoanalyst Looks at the Super-natural. Nandor Fodor New York: Garrett Publications

14. Girod Sr., Robert J.-Infamous: Murders and Mysteries: cold case files (2009) iUniverse

15. The Detroit news" Woman's trip to tragedy is retraced on Mackinac page 1A, July 30, 1960

16. Gringhuis, Dirk -Were-wolves and Will-o-the-wisps: French takes of Mackinac Retold, Mackinac Island State Park Commission (1974)

17. Kane,Grace F.-Myths and Legends of The Mackinaws (1887) Black Letter Press, Grand Rapids, MI

Acknowledgements

TO THOSE WHO ENTERED MY life, for however brief a moment, and roused me from my human slumber by sharing their special gifts of knowledge, support and understanding, bestowing upon me a bit of their magic: Rosie, Bea, Warren, Pat, and Bonnie-who in her indomitable way opened a door that led to my wonderful adventures. I thank you.

My special thanks and gratitude go to Robb Kaczor, for his vital contributions and involvement with this project. He is indeed the Ghost Hunting King!

My thanks to those that came before me insisting paranormal phenomena exists on Mackinac Island, and wrote about it.

Thanks to The City of St. Ignace, Mackinac State Historic Parks, The Mackinac Island Library, The St Ignace Library, The Mackinac Island Tourism Bureau for the information they provided.